For Meredith,

Alfred Winter,

Warmest regards.

DISCOVER YOUR REAL ASSETS

ALFRED UHLER

Discover Your

REAL
ASSETS

*"Man will become better when
you show him what he is like."*

—ANTON CHEKHOV

NEW YORK: THE CITADEL PRESS

PUBLISHED UNDER THE AUSPICES OF
THE DAVID SEABURY SCHOOL

CONTENTS

INTRODUCTION

Here *you* are! I have never seen you, probably never heard of you. Yet within this book you will find a description of yourself. Not, perhaps, as you are at this moment, but *you* as you can be, as you want to be. To help you find out just what that Self of yours is and what it can do is the object of this book.

Let me say at the outset that you will find nothing negative about yourself, for there is nothing negative in the Self your Creator gave you. We shall help you find your real assets.

There's no mystery about it, no soothsaying. It is according to a scientific principle. You know that a rose is a rose, but there are Crimson Glory roses, Ophelia roses, Rosa Rugosa, Floribunda, and many more. A dog is a dog, but there are collies and spaniels and Scotties and Bedlingtons and dachsunds, to name a few. And you'd never mistake one for the other.

You know that every race of man has its distinctive characteristics, some more easily discerned than others.

Well, there are also types of human personalities that you will find to be distinctive psychologically when you learn what their differences are. Because the human is a more complex organism than other forms of life the variations are more subtle. But these can be defined, and as you learn what they are you will not only find that you know how your own particular type of mind works but you will also be able to see what makes other people tick.

Of course every person is unique. No one just like you has ever been or ever will be. But in your quality of mind and emotion you fall into a specific grouping. This quality is inborn. It never changes. It can be developed, as it should be, or it can be inhibited. This is the result of the impact of the environment.

Various psychologists, notably Carl Jung and Ernst Kretschmer, have made type classifications. David Seabury, the pioneer consulting psychologist, has embodied some of their ideas in his type classification, particularly Kretschmer's concept of cycloid and schizoid. But Seabury has gone into the type differentiations much more fully; hence his classification is very much more specific.

Seabury had many thousands of clients when he was practicing in New York. In his work with them he found that there were certain basic characteristics which each one possessed, according to his emotional drive. The latter fell into four large groupings, based on the four instinctual drives of *attraction, curiosity, pugnacity* and *flight*. In man, these instincts are sublimated.

Attraction or sex, the instinct of creation and nurture, produces the physical infant; in its sublimated form, it produces the brain child, the book, the work of art, the invention, the new in any field.

The drive of *curiosity* becomes wonder, the urge to know why, what, how and when, but particularly why. People of this type are especially interested in the *meaning* of what happens, rather than the simple fact.

The *pugnacity* instinct becomes rage, the constructive urge, the drive to change things. It finds its outlet in building, in various branches of engineering, and so forth.

The instinct of *flight* takes the form of caution, foresight. It looks ahead, it conserves, it senses values. It takes care of things and people.

So Seabury calls the four basic emotional drives *Sex, Wonder, Rage* and *Fear*. Everyone has all four of them, but one is accented in each individual.

Seabury also found that everyone has a secondary drive which modifies the first. For example, in every Sex type person, the creative drive is modified by wonder, rage or fear. Therefore he calls them respectively *Sex-wonder, Sex-rage* and *Sex-fear*.

In the *Sex-wonder* type, the wonder deepens the creativity, tending to send it into more philosophic areas.

In *Sex-rage*, the rage, the urge to do, drives the creativity on to fulfillment.

In *Sex-fear*, the caution tends to retard the creativity, to keep it from believing that it is creative.

Thus each primary drive is modified by one of the other three, giving us *Wonder-sex, Wonder-rage, Wonder-fear;*

Rage-sex, Rage-wonder, Rage-fear;

Fear-sex, Fear-wonder, Fear-rage.

These are all described at length in succeeding chapters.

No one drive is more important than any other. Each has its particular work to do in the world, work for which it is especially designed. When functioning properly, each one cooperates with the others. The creative, sex drive gets the idea out of the blue; the wonder drive interprets it, forms the blueprint; the rage drive builds according to the blueprint, the fear drive raises the necessary cash, insures the creation, and in general takes over and sells the finished product.

You have one of these drives accented, and you will recognize your basic type in the description of it. There are tests, too, which will help you to pinpoint your type. When you know it, you will know where to put your efforts. You will know, too, why you have not been satisfied with your life up to now. You will know why you have felt instant rapport with some people and not with others.

In Dr. Seabury's work and in my own, I have seen over and over again the exhilarating effect of applying this knowledge of the types to individual cases. A man will enter the consulting room looking despondent and unhappy, his face a mask of gloom. He isn't satisfied with his work or with his life. Nothing gives him happiness.

First I find out what his type is. When I know that, I can give him a picture of what his native capacities are, the kind of life to which he is best suited.

He has undoubtedly thought himself a failure. And he has been, because he's been trying to do something for which he wasn't fitted. He didn't know *himself*.

As I describe the man he really is, his face lights up. He grows excited about the possibilities opening up before him. Hope springs within him, and he leaves the office with head up, firm step, and a smile. The new picture he has of himself is stimulating and inspiring.

You, too, can have this experience. The reward which the knowledge of the types offers is a new view of yourself, and I can promise you that you will like what you see.

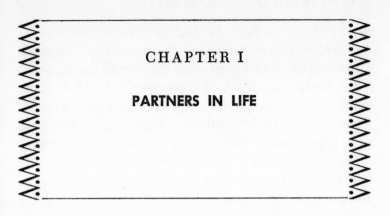

CHAPTER I

PARTNERS IN LIFE

Before I go into a detailed description of the individual types, I want to describe certain characteristics which are common to several types.

These are the *extravert-introvert* classification and the *cycloid-schizoid* grouping, which I shall take up in this chapter, and the *will* accent which will be described in Chapter II.

Extravert and introvert are terms much used today, and much abused! So let's define the terms. The difference lies in the way in which the *attention* of the person functions.

The *extravert's* attention is broad, horizontal, relatively shallow. He sees everything in his environment. For instance, when he has been in a room for awhile, he can tell you everything that is in it. This comprehensive, broad attention has definite values.

The *introvert's* attention, on the other hand, is deep and vertical. It is selective, picking out one or two objects from many. These he sees in great detail. If he were in the same room with the extrovert, he couldn't tell what was in it except for the one or two things that caught his attention. These he'd know a lot more about than would the extravert.

In general, this is why the introvert is likely to know more about the people he meets than does the extravert. Each person who interests him receives deep attention, so he might possibly discover some of their inner secrets.

Six of the twelve emotional types are extraverts, six introverts; all fear and wonder types are extraverts, rage and sex types introverts.

There is another classification which is frequently confused with the extravert-introvert grouping. This is what the German psychologist Ernst Kretschmer calls the *cyloid-schizoid classification*. Don't be afraid of those words—you'll find them very useful in analyzing yourself and other people, as soon as you get the picture of what they mean. *They have no abnormal connotation whatsoever*—they are symptoms of health, not of disease.

The *cycloid's* mind is logical. He consciously takes the facts as he finds them, analyzes, classifies, compares them consciously, and comes to a logical conclusion. His interest is in method and procedure. He is stimulated by his environment, and wants to affect it in some way. He is a realist, not much interested in ideas per se. His attitude is, "Let's get busy and *do* something." He depends on his environment to stimulate his thought. What people say or do, what has happened in the world, the advantage of one article or line of approach over another are the types of things he needs to get him going. He's interested in the fact itself, not particularly in its meaning. In choosing a career, he tends to prefer work in a large organization, and likes to follow a routine. He generally has hosts of friends, loves parties, and doesn't like to be alone for long.

The *schizoid's* mind works in just the opposite way. He is perhaps the least understood of the human family. He is often considered impractical, illogical, up in the clouds. As we understand how his mind works naturally, we see why this is so. He is primarily a thinker, a man of ideas. His thinking originates in his own stream of consciousness. He doesn't need outside events to start his thinking process. He is interested not in affecting his environment, but in the way his environment affects him. He is preoccupied with what he thinks about life, the objects and events around him, and what to do about them. His reasoning we call analogical. This means that he takes in the facts, objects and events unconsciously. His senses convey these immediately to his unconscious. There they are analyzed, classified and criticised in relation to both his personal unconscious and the race mind. His conclusion then leaps full-blown into consciousness, as inspiration or intuition. Since the whole operation has taken place in his unconscious, he probably cannot tell immediately what the factors were that produced his conclusion. He is sure that it is valid, and it may actually be more so than that of the logical thinker, because both conscious and unconscious factors have gone into its making. But you can see why he is often at a loss in an argument with a cycloid, for he may not be able to give a point-by-point proof of the validity of his stand. He is a lone wolf, wanting to work for himself rather than in an organization. He dislikes routine in any area. He has a few close friends, doesn't care much for crowds, and needs to be alone part of the time.

Now in every undertaking there are two main parts. First there is the idea, the concept. Second, there is the putting of that concept into practical form of some sort. Both parts are necessary in the work of the world.

The schizoid's characteristics make him best fitted for the first part, while the cycloid is better adapted to the second. When the two types get together on this basis, all is as it should be, as it was planned by the great Planner. Each type is necessary to the other, and necessary to life. When both recognize this, and each respects the other's contribution to the overall picture, much friction, competition and anger will be eliminated.

One of the problems in education is that it is so often geared entirely to the cycloid mind, that is, the mind that emphasizes facts and proofs more than ideas. However, the best teaching always seeks to find the meaning behind the facts.

You can see how this difference in temperament produces misunderstanding and conflict. The hopeful thing is that now we do know the cause of the confusion, and can do something about it. When the cycloid knows what motivates the mind of the schizoid, and vice versa, human relations will be put on a much more scientific basis. These are *natural* ways in which the individual's mind works.

Work aptitudes vary greatly along this great division of cycloid and schizoid. In general, the schizoid is a lone wolf, liking to work by himself, not liking to take orders as to how he shall do a job. So he is found more generally in the professions, such as medicine, the ministry, psychology, teaching, research, exploration, and all the arts.

The cycloid temperament is better qualified for success

in business, engineering, trade, manufacturing, transportation, salesmanship, banking, insurance, and so forth.

But both cycloids and schizoids can operate on any one of the planes of life. Gandhi, for example, was a cycloid on a very high plane. It was his cycloid emphasis on method and procedure that enabled him to work out the process of constructive non-resistance which freed India. Beethoven, another cycloid, developed the form of the symphony, and Bach, still another cycloid, invented the fugue, a difficult procedure for any composer. Brahms, on the other hand, wrote beautiful music but never concerned himself with evolving new procedures.

Not long ago I finished a questionnaire designed to select boys for certain professions. What was wanted was a method of picking candidates especially fitted for law, medicine, and engineering. In other words, the person who asked for the questionnaire wanted boys who were interested in working for themselves, not as cogs in the wheels of a big organization. What did this mean? I had to slant my tests to sift out the schizoids from the group tested. For these are the ones who prefer lone wolf jobs.

Some years ago I had a very interesting case. A woman from the Middle West came to see me about her son. She and her husband were both schizoids, deeply interested in ideas. They were very intelligent, but their son puzzled them.

He loved to hang around the town garage and help the mechanics with the motors. The parents didn't approve of this at all. They naturally expected the boy to be interested in ideas, as they were. They expected him to go to college. But he rebelled.

I explained the cycloid-schizoid difference to the

mother. I pointed out that her boy was probably a cycloid, so that the kind of life she and her husband preferred left the son quite cold. I told her that if they forced him to the life they had planned for him, he would never be happy or successful. She saw immediately that it was necessary to go with the boy's love. So he was given the kind of training that would fit him for the life he wanted.

Years ago a schizoid came to see me. He had spent his business life in mechanical and executive jobs. Although he had been successful, he had disliked every minute of it. When I told him that he was creative he was greatly surprised, but very pleased.

On the basis of my diagnosis of his type, he began to look for a creative job where he could be his own boss. Finally, he found one in which he had complete charge of one phase of the business and needed his creativity every day. He is a changed and happy man.

Several years ago I received a letter from a man in England. He had read a book of mine which had made a great impression on him. He wanted to know why the psychiatrists in England didn't have a psychology like David Seabury's. Then he asked me if it were possible for me to help him. Well, it was a large order.

I sent him my book on vocational guidance, and he completed the tests in it. These showed that he was a schizoid introvert. This gave me the clue to his general reactions.

His father had left him a large grocery and butcher shop. Apparently in England it is still the practice for the son to follow his father's business. The shop was successful, but he hated it. I was able to explain to him the basic reasons for his distaste. I also advised him to look for work more adapted to his creative nature.

The last time I heard from him he had put his shop up for sale, and planned to go into housing. He had always loved to design houses, which would give him an outlet for his basic nature.

You see how the temperamental differences affect the choice of a career. They also play a vital role in the family relations. Here usually there are both cycloids and schizoids. Mother tends to understand and therefore like Betsy, because she is a cycloid as Mother is. Susy, a schizoid, doesn't fare so well because Mother doesn't understand the way her mind works. This we call biological rejection. The child feels the lack of understanding as a lack of love, though it isn't necessarily so. Mothers don't usually want to reject their children, or have the children *feel* rejected, which is another thing. When this knowledge of the difference in temperament is more widely disseminated the problem will be largely eliminated.

I know a couple in which the wife is a cycloid, the husband schizoid. Both are on fairly high planes of life. When they were young they were passionately in love.

This marriage has been happier than most, yet even here the difference in the way the two look at life has affected it adversely. The wife is a most loving individual, generous, of the highest character. She has hosts of friends, and loves to be on the go. But her mind does not go beyond her social life.

Her husband is deeply interested in ideas but he cannot interest her in any of them. She can talk well about events of everyday life, what people said or did, and draw her conclusions from them. But she is not interested in ideas for the sake of ideas.

She loves her husband, but cannot understand how he can be so impractical in his thinking. His mystic religious leaning she cannot understand. It doesn't make sense to her. "What is the use of it?" she wonders.

Her husband loves her, and indulges her, but he cannot help but feel frustrated that he cannot discuss his ideas with her, that they are not basically interested in the same things. As he has become older, his subjective feeling has grown stronger, so they have inevitably grown somewhat apart.

They respect each other's way of thinking, but do not think together. The fact that they do know about this cycloid-schizoid difference has greatly helped to alleviate the schism between them.

The story of the ugly duckling, like all good fairy tales, has psychic meaning. You remember the mother duck hatched a brood of ducklings. But among them was an awkward, long-necked bird which they all thought quite ugly, because it was so different. Certainly it was not like a duck. But when the little bird grew up, it turned out to be a swan. This is a poetic picture of the difference in temperament and the criticism it produces.

Rejection is always present in any neurosis. When the child thinks he is rejected, he believes it is his fault. He is sure he is no good and that nobody loves him. The rejected person goes out into life carrying this pattern of rejection with him. He expects to be rejected, in whatever situation he finds himself.

The fact that the feeling of rejection is so often based on this temperamental difference between parent and child is a compelling reason why the information about it should be widely disseminated.

The sex, or creative, drive and the wonder drive make up the schizoid grouping, while the rage and fear drives are cycloids.

We meet cycloids and schizoids every day of our lives. Each has to be handled differently. The approach which will succeed with a cycloid will fail with a schizoid. Knowing the aspects and tendencies of each will add greatly to your success in human relations and consequent happiness in life.

Now we are going to get a little more complicated. But as we go along, you'll see how it works out.

We've said that the extravert-introvert classification is a matter of *attention*, the extravert paying attention to the broad picture, the introvert focussing on a limited area but going deeply into it.

The cycloid-schizoid grouping has to do with the individual's *relation* to his environment. The cycloid is stimulated by his environment and wants to affect it. The schizoid is stimulated by his own stream of consciousness, and is interested in the way his environment affects him.

Thus, we have certain types that are *cycloid extraverts*. That is, they need the stimulation of their environment and want to affect it in some way. Their attention is on the broad picture of their environment. They are realists, generally practical, so-called. These are the *Fear* types, in the Seabury terminology.

Then we have *cycloid introverts*. These are also stimulated by their environment and interested in changing it. But their attention is deep rather than broad, concentrating on a limited area rather than on the broad picture. These, too, are realists. They the *Rage* types.

The third group are the *schizoid extraverts*. Their attention is broad—each sees everything in his setting. But he functions from the stimulus of his own stream of consciousness, and is not dependent on his environment to stimulate him. He is interested in the meaning of events, rather than in the facts per se. These individuals are the *Wonder* types.

Fourth is the *schizoid introvert*. He is stimulated by his own stream of consciousness rather than by external events. He is interested in how his environment affects him rather than in affecting his environment. He differs from the wonder type, schizoid extraverts, in that his attention is deep rather than broad. He sees deeply into a limited area rather than getting the broad picture. This Seabury calls the *Sex* type.

Following are chapters which describe each type in detail, also charts which show their relationship with each other. Let me repeat—no one type is any better, any superior, to any other. Each was designed to fill a certain need in the world.

CHAPTER II

YOU HAVE A BASIC "WILL" ACCENT

I am going to take up next what Seabury calls your *will* accent. This is the way in which your emotions affect your thought and action, and the way your combined thought and emotion make you go into action in life.

There are three ways in which your *will* may go into action. While everyone has all three, one is always accented. Seabury calls the three wills the *imperative,* the *deliberative,* and the *adaptive.* No one *will* type is better than any other. They are different, that is all. Each one has its advantage, and is suited to a particular need.

If your *will* is *imperative* your mind acts very quickly, the fastest of the three types. You know immediately what you think in any situation. You arrive at your conclusions with the speed of thought, and you tend to act on your conclusions immediately. You are likely to be impatient with people of other types because they don't "get" things as rapidly as you do. You may think them stupid. That in itself may possibly cause you trouble in your human relations. Because your conclusions come so quickly and seem so right to you, other people may think you are bossy, although you do not mean to be and are not aware of their feelings.

If you are *deliberative*, it takes time for you to make up your mind. You want to weigh all the factors involved so that you can arrive at a calm, judicial conclusion. If you are asked to decide something immediately, you don't want to answer. But if you must, you may want to change your decision the next day. People sometimes, for this reason, think you are stubborn, or changeable, whereas you are simply acting according to the dictates of your nature.

If you are *adaptive*, you know immediately what you think in any situation, but don't mention it until you know how others feel. You adapt to them, in other words. Sometimes you make difficulties for yourself because you say *yes* when you wanted to say *no*. You let yourself be drawn into situations by your desire to please others. You may even agree with the man who criticises you! That is, at first. You come to a true evaluation later.

You can see how this difference in basic *will* types affects human relations. It probably causes more trouble than any other psychological factor. The imperative gets impatient with the deliberative for not being quicker; the deliberative thinks the imperative can't be right because he's always making snap decisions; the adaptive gets into jams because, in his desire to please, he sometimes agrees with too many people, or with the wrong ones. When you know that each person was born with his particular *will* type, that he isn't trying to be bossy, or stubborn, or changeable, you accept his way of reacting without getting mad at him for it. And more than all else, you recognize your own type. You see how you may be getting in someone else's hair, and so try to modify your own reactions.

It is easy to see how an imperative boss can make life miserable for a deliberative employee and consider the employee stupid, when he is just being deliberative. The boss expects Miss Stone to be ready on the jump the minute he is ready to dictate. Why can't she find that letter he gave her to file yesterday? He forgets that he told her there was no hurry about it, so she had put it aside to file when she had more time.

And of course the reverse is true. An imperative woman I know worked in a large bank. Her immediate superior was deliberative. She'd arrive promptly every morning, and so would he. But it took him two full hours to go through his mail, deciding deliberately what to do with each item. Meantime she'd sit twiddling her thumbs impatiently, or try to find something to do to fill time. She cleaned her desk so often she practically wore the paint off.

Finally her superior would hand her a sheaf of stock market quotations to look up. She went to it immediately, and finished the job rapidly. When she gave her findings to her superior, he always said, sometimes quite irritably, "What, finished so soon? I thought it would take you all day!" Then he'd put the quotations on his desk. By the time he got around to working with them they were obsolete and she had to do the work all over again.

In my practice I have known cases where an adaptive has said yes—and gotten himself married! He knew the girl wanted to marry him, and he didn't want to hurt her feelings. So he got married, and lived to repent his adaptiveness. It's much harder on both parties to divorce than for him to say no in the first place. But the adaptive sometimes has to learn the hard way.

Jim W. is imperative, his wife Gloria deliberative. He's a successful business man, and in the way of many such, thinks his success in business proves that he knows best about everything. His imperative nature magnifies his self-assurance.

One night they were sitting reading. Suddenly Jim shut his book and announced, "I've decided we're going to Florida on Friday." Immediately he picked up the phone and called the railroad for tickets and the hotel for reservations. All the time Gloria was vainly trying to get his ear. She didn't know whether she could get ready by Friday. In fact, she was not sure that she wanted to go to Florida at all. She was busy thinking of all the reasons against going. Anyway, she needed time to sleep on it.

At last she managed to get in her protests, between Jim's phone calls. He was very angry. What was the matter with her, anyway? Wasn't it nice to go to Florida in the winter? Wasn't he doing a generous thing for her? He didn't say it in so many words, but he plainly implied that she was pretty stupid.

She wanted to make her own decision, in her own time. She should have been consulted before he bought the tickets, not after. She thought of all the times her husband had been wrong. "Snap decisions," she thought scornfully.

So pretty soon there was a knock-down and drag-out argument, one of a long, long series. Both were acting as their will types dictated, but neither knew it.

A certain man I know is adaptive. He is delightful to be with, because he is so agreeable. Whatever I say he agrees with immediately, and repeats the phrase I've used in the most approving manner. He makes me feel that every word I say is pure gold, and seems completely convinced. You can see why I find him a most delightful companion!

However, over the years I've discovered that I'm not the only one he adapts to. He also agrees with others whose ideas are diametrically opposed to mine. He's like a chameleon, changing his ideas with every passing shadow.

As you can see, the knowledge of the will types sheds a great light on human reactions. I've never yet had a client who didn't react immediately to my description of the will types. "Haven't you seen this type in action?" I ask. And the answer invariably is, "I certainly have."

Let me say that this analysis of the will types is not yet a matter of general knowledge. Many a psychologist will tell you that there is no such condition, because he doesn't know about it. He will also tell you that there is no such thing as emotional types of personality, because he hasn't been taught anything about them. As I said in the Introduction, Jung and Kretschmer have evolved type classifications, but in my opinion they are not as specific as those Seabury has discovered. Anyone who has studied these as I have and has seen how accurately they work out does not have the slightest doubt of their validity. They explain basic human personality as it has never been explained before.

To recapitulate: In general, the *imperative* is the quick, sometimes arbitrary, will. It is tactical rather than strategic. That is, it is good where quick decisions are called for, rather than for long-range planning.

The *deliberative* is the strategic will. It waits until enough facts have been learned to give it the basis for a considered opinion.

The *adaptive* is the politic will, always trying to please. It can become the dupe of those with more decided opinions.

Each emotional type has its specific will type, so you will be hearing more about these in later chapters.

Meantime, you can use to advantage what you've already learned, in seeing yourself and in seeing the other people in your environment.

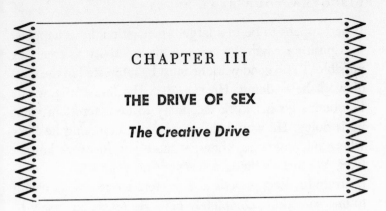

CHAPTER III

THE DRIVE OF SEX

The Creative Drive

Your drive is an expression of emotion. All your emotions are your dynamic. They are the urges of your organism. They flow into thought, motivate it and give it power. Your thought receives the impact of the drive. Its function is to direct that drive, to show it what it can do, where it can go, what it had better not do. It is the guide of the emotion. That is thought's only power. You can see, therefore, the importance of learning all you can about these loves and capacities of yours. For they are, in reality, you, your very life force.

I am going to tell you first about the *creative drive*. This springs from the animal instinct of attraction, and can be sublimated to the spiritual level of feeling and thought. Seabury calls this the *sex drive*. In this type, the creativity is completely original. It is not modified by any existing idea, object, or relationship of ideas or objects. The creative type is likely to be this kind of person—he dislikes any routine work, and dislikes to take orders from anyone. In whatever he does, he prefers a lone wolf job.

If he happens to be in a large organization, he is happiest in a position where he can use his creativity as freely as possible. To do good work he must be interested in the kind of work he is doing. He considers the financial rewards he obtains for his work secondary to his interest in what he is doing. He would rather work at something he likes where the pay is less than get more pay for work he dislikes. When he's doing something he enjoys he can concentrate for long periods at a stretch. He is always trying to find something completely new. He reacts adversely to old ideas, or to doing things in the prescribed way. What he is really doing is to find the higher action of any law.

His ideas come to him in an analogical way. This means that he reasons through inspiration, intuition, or hunch. All his analyzing, classifying, and criticising are done in his unconscious. So the conclusion that comes to his conscious mind is full-blown. He is sure that his idea is right, but he is unable to tell you the steps which make him sure of this. A person of this type is often at a loss in argument with someone whose mind works by controlled association. But he can always work out the reasons for his conclusion. This he has to do later, rather than at the moment. In other words, his conclusion comes to him first. Then he has to go back and substantiate it.

The emotions of the creative type are quick and jagged. On hearing sad news his spirits immediately hit bottom. The reverse is true when he hears good news. His emotions are so near the surface that he is likely to err on the side of too much feeling. He is therefore not the type you expect to organize either people or things. Because of his analogical reasoning, he is often considered by the world to be impractical and unsound in his thought. But this is not true.

The creative type is full of nurture for others. These people respond immediately and sympathetically to suffering, injustice, and inequity. Some of this group are far away from creativity on a material plane. They will be found in pure philosophy, pure science, art, music, sculpture, drama, poetry. While these activities do not seem to be necessary for the physical survival of the race, they are very important for its spiritual survival.

The purely creative type gets his ideas out of the blue. He asks, seeks, and knocks at the gate of his soul, desiring the inflow of feeling and thought. First, the desire, the urge, comes. Then the period of listening until the idea takes form. When it does, the imagination plays with it, finding out what to do with it. Then reason picks out what is practical. Next comes the judgment, which chooses the way of thought and feeling most appealing to this particular creative mind. And in that judgment there is always a conviction that what is being written or painted or carved or otherwise produced is deeply true. For this is the way in which the love which motivates the creative type finds its form of manifestation.

For the first thirty-five years of my own life, I was completely ignorant of the fact that I was creative or that there was such a thing as creativity. I had never come in contact with it. To be a banker was the only ideal occupation for a man that had been given me. So when David Seabury told me, in my first meeting with him, that I was a creative type, I was delighted. (You see, he was using psychosynthesis with me.) We discussed what I should do. He advised my going home and spending an

hour every day in creativity of some sort. He explained
that all the loves and abilities which God had given me
were supposed to be used, and that the reason why I
had had to come to him was that I was not using them.
Hence I was completely frustrated, without knowing why.
He said, "If you don't use your abilities, they will abuse
you." There was never a truer word said than that. I went
home and followed his advice. I began to create, and
found great joy in doing so. This affected my whole life,
in all areas, positively.

The pure creative drive can be expressed in almost
any kind of way. One sex type can be writing a novel,
while another is inventing a machine. Another may be
breeding dogs or plants, another may be inventing some
new business method. Any aspect of life may receive the
attention of the creative person and stimulate him.

Alexander Graham Bell was a creative mind on the
objective or material plane. His father and grandfather
had been teachers of the deaf and dumb. Bell was brought
up to be interested in helping the unfortunate. This was
his main purpose in life. He was certainly a most spiritual
man.

He was born in Edinburgh, but finally got to Boston.
There he met two prominent citizens, both of whom
had deaf and dumb daughters. They engaged him to work
with the girls, and he lived at the Saunders' home. While
there, he worked on what he called the harmonic tele-
graph to help the deaf. He knew a lot about acoustics, but
apparently not too much about electricity. Saunders and
Hubbard, the two fathers, backed him financially while
he worked on this project. But he suddenly abandoned it.
For he acquired a human ear from a cadaver, and studied

and analyzed it carefully. From this study, the idea of the telephone first burst into his mind.

That's the way the creative imagination works. The message from the Universal Mind is received; the creative mind takes note of it, and develops a strong conviction. Then the creative mind has to go back and find the steps leading to the conclusion. It was a long time before Bell and Thomas Watson, his collaborator, actually heard sounds transmitted over the wire, but eventually they did. The first words were Bell's, saying, "Come here, Watson, I want you." Neither money nor power were of any importance to Bell. It was the spiritual motivation of helping his fellow man which actuated everything he did.

Robert Fulton, the inventor of the steamboat, was also a very creative person. He was an artist, and at first painting took up most of his attention. He became one of the best painters in America. He studied in Paris, and did many well-known portraits. But in his mind for years had been the intuitional picture or belief that boats could be made to run on steam power. He spent a long time in experimentation before he was able to put his dream into action. But finally the day arrived, and the *Claremont* was ready to sail. It steamed from New York to Claremont on the Hudson River, then went to Albany, a hundred and fifty miles, in thirty-two hours. Fulton's main motivation was the joy of creation, and not the idea of making money.

Lionel Feininger was a creative type in painting. He might be called a poet in paint. His works have a deep serenity, and light is handled in the most beautiful, dramatic way. His art is abstract; a feeling of peace is given you as you look at the lovely designs.

David Seabury was a creative type in philosophy and

psychology. His mind was continually searching for new aspects of truth and new meanings of life. His discovery of the four basic drives, which is the subject of this book, is a fine example of his endeavor to help his fellow man through his creativity. For this is an entirely new idea, and one of the first ways ever arrived at of defining emotion.

Lewis Carroll was a creative type whose profession was teaching mathematics at Oxford. While he undoubtedly was interested in math, on which subject he had written several books, there was a vein of creative humor in him that is unique in all literature. Who but Carroll would have thought of the SyZyGy Waltz, or written to a little girl asking her how she'd like to dance the Lobster Quadrille with him?

I know a man of this type who found himself early in life with a large family to support. He could not do this on the money he could make in art work, which was his field. So against his will and his nature, he was forced to take a job in a great organization that had no relation to art whatever. He has stuck to this all his life, although he has a great aversion for it. But the admirable thing about this creative man, and the thing which actually has saved his life, is the fact that he never gave up his creativity. Every spare moment of his life is given to his art work. He works evenings, Saturdays, Sundays and holidays. And the results of this devotion to the needs of his first nature, to his loves, to the God within him, are beautiful works of art. Had he not been faithful to the demands of his loves, it is doubtful whether he would have lived. God is not fooling—you must treat your loves with respect—or else.

While creativity is found everywhere, you will find the type more frequently in the arts and the professions. This is because these are generally lone wolf jobs. The doctor of medicine is his own boss, as is the psychologist, the teacher (to some degree), the minister, the priest, the rabbi. The theater, radio, television, movies, acting, newspaper work and magazines offer work that the creative type likes.

The sex type is very loving and responsive to love. These people are outgoing to others, spontaneous, and usually with a strong dynamic. So they naturally work well with others except in the area of career. Here, while they try to get along with other people, it may be at great cost to their own creativity.

The sex type is a good teacher, if the subject interests him. He is especially interested in human nature and its well-being. You will not find the same executive power in him that other types exhibit. Nor will you think of him as particularly practical or efficient.

The imagination of the type is creative, the ideas always new and original. The imagination and reason prefer to play with ideas rather than with more objective concepts. The reason of the type is productive. This is a sensing of trends, tendencies, implications, significances. By intuition they sense the meaning of world events, and they feel keenly the currents of world feeling and tension. They perceive and feel the latent content in all that passes before their eyes. They realize the inside when they perceive the outside.

This is why they are found so often in the arts of every variety. The artist is the seer of the new, the prophet who foretells the way the future is going. He, more than any other type, allows his mind to open to guidance from the spirit, and so is able to produce in his work the new face the spirit is showing in his age.

There are two kinds of creativity, spiritual creativity and material creativity. Let us take the material, objective variety first. I conceive the idea that I would like to build a table. My love of construction is the motive power. Love always comes first. I begin to conceive the form of table I desire. I see the top in my mind, and then the base (or vice-versa). It's now in the dream stage, or formative degree. My love is satisfied with the form and gives me the go-ahead. The table is all in the love and thought stage up to this point.

Now is the stage of matter, manifestation of the loved idea. I am down to the point of method and procedure. Now I draw the table to measurement—length, breadth, height, proportion. I design the turnings for the legs; I decide on the wood I shall use. Now I put together the actual table. My love has been satisfied as I look with love upon my creation.

The process of creativity is always the feeling, or love, first. Then comes the second, or forming stage, of thought; then the third stage, the object itself. The original love has been put into form.

The purely creative type creates in all fields. He may be a businessman like J. P. Morgan the elder, who created the idea of the corporation. This was a new concept in the conduct of business. He may be like David Sarnoff, head of the Radio Corporation of America. He is a sex type with a mind that is always aware of trends. He is always prophesying what is going to happen in the next decade. His mind is continually playing with new ideas for the industry.

He may be a writer like Thomas Wolfe. He was able to reproduce the impressions life made on him so vividly that they reach out of the book and pull the reader along. There is nothing logical about this thought. It is full of feeling, intuitive and inspirational. His work is a far cry from the practical creativity of Morgan, yet they are both sex or creative types.

Creativity is the best expression there is of surprise in life. For to be interesting life must furnish surprises. Imagine the boredom of a life where everything could be foreseen! No one would want such a life if it were offered to him. It is the creativity of man that adds so much to the enjoyment of life, not to speak of the many objects of new use it produces.

The sex types are not all the same. They differ in other, more fundamental ways than in the area of their creativity. The difference is caused by the modifying type. That is, we have the sex drive modified by the constructive urge, or by the interpretive drive, or by the urge of caution, sense perception. These we call respectively *sex-rage, sex-wonder* and *sex-fear*. In the succeeding chapters I shall discuss the three variations of creativity.

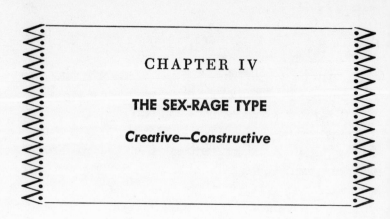

CHAPTER IV

THE SEX-RAGE TYPE

Creative—Constructive

In the *sex-rage* type, the creativity is modified by rage or the constructive, mechanical sense. Here the creativity is pushed along by the modifier. The rage doesn't inhibit the creativity; it drives it along uncritically.

I consider this of all types the natural leader of man. It is not that the sex-rage person demands leadership. He simply is the kind of man whom people naturally look to in a crisis. The man who most effectively demonstrated leadership par excellence was Winston Churchill. He is a sex-rage type. With the chips down, and everything at the lowest ebb of fortune in the early days of the last war, he naturally stepped in, and with indomitable courage and determination pulled England and the world to victory. Can anyone ever forget that cheerful face and the V-for-Victory sign of his raised fingers? He epitomized leadership, leadership that men conferred upon him. It was anything but dictatorial. Over and over again, the British tried to get along without him. But he soon was leading them again. They had to come to him.

Society always needs leaders. There must be a head of any organization, large or small. When they are chosen as Churchill was, because of his own magnitude, so that all can see, all is well. But when they push themselves up, and seize power for themselves secretly and cruelly, as Stalin did, then the act is against nature and very dangerous. Needless to say Stalin was not a sex-rage type, a natural leader.

Churchill displays creativity to a pronounced degree. His was the name behind the task, his the concept of the Gallipoli campaign, which now is seen as a great plan badly executed. His mind was full of ideas for new campaigns, never without a concept of what to do next. His generals didn't like this creativity of his. But he always won his point, and then they carried on. He was the prophet of the air age. He was always able to sense world trends and feelings years ahead, and his prophecies have always been fulfilled. He is always noble in everything he says and does. His is the great mind, able to perceive the qualities of the great scene.

And of course his inimitable humor is inherent in this type, for the sex-rage person always sees things in an unexpected way. Churchill, being a genius, has humor, wit, irony, and satire. No phase of humor escapes him. The usual sex-rage humor is puckish, childlike and elfishly delightful. Churchill, it is said, when returning home after an absence enters the hall and barks like a dog. His wife immediately knows he has arrived.

There is a story told about Phillips Brooks, the prominent Episcopalian clergyman in Boston, which illustrates sex-rage humor. He told his congregation that a little boy had come to try to sell him three newborn kittens.

The boy said, "They're good Episcopalian kittens, Dr. Brooks." But Brooks said he didn't believe he was in need of any kittens right then. A short time later, the boy appeared at the home of Edward Everett Hale, who had a Unitarian church near by. He offered the kittens to Dr. Hale, saying, "They're good Unitarian kittens, Dr. Hale." "Why," expostulated Dr. Hale, "I understand you told Dr. Brooks last week that they were good Episcopalian kittens." "Oh yes, they were then," replied the boy, "but since then they've had their eyes opened."

Usually the type doesn't impress you with its intellect. While sex-rage types are just as intelligent as other people on their plane of life, or more so, you never think of them as "brains." Wonder seems to be a problem to them. They are not usually able to probe into the deepest meanings.

When they lend their talents to business, they usually attain positions of leadership. They like lone wolf jobs, where they can use their creativity, and not have someone telling them what to do. They feel that they know what to do in any situation.

J. P. Morgan, Senior, was this type. Everything he did was on a big scale. He was a leader from the beginning. He never seemed to go through any apprenticeship. His creativity showed itself, as I said in the last chapter, in his invention of the idea of the corporation.

The type likes to do things in a lordly way. They are lavish. There is a bigness of spirit about them. "I command" illustrates their attitude toward life. They are inclined to stand a little apart from the herd, although they are perfectly generous in their response to another's need.

They do not easily express their deeper feelings, and almost never "slop over." But the dramatic is very strong in them. They made great tragedians like Edwin Booth, Fredric March, Laurence Olivier. Sarah Bernhardt, Marilyn Monroe, June Allyson are examples on the feminine side.

The children of the type are usually exceptionally fearless in a physical way. They can, however, become quite fearful psychically, because they are so sensitive. Their emotions range from a great gaiety to a tremendous somberness when they are down. They resemble what New Englanders call "an open and shet day," when cloud masses darken the scene and then suddenly the sun breaks through. There's nothing gradual about these natures. Their changes from elation to depression are abrupt. They like familiar surroundings. The same chair, the same room, the same locality, seem to give them a sense of security. It's a kind of pussycat quality.

Some of them look like pussycats, too. This characteristic of the type was recognized in the name given to Clemenceau, "The Tiger." He became the leader of France in its greatest moments. Like Churchill, and in the tradition of the type, he had no sense of physical fear.

When the Germans broke through, in their last drive, the situation for the Allies was so serious that Churchill went to France himself, to help in the crisis. There the two sex-rage types got together and went to the front. With shells bursting all around them, they both had a wonderful time. Finally Churchill had to suggest that they leave. Clemenceau showed no indication of ever retiring from the battle.

Like Churchill, Clemenceau was a most extraordinary

fighter. Neither ever knew when he was licked—so he never was. Clemenceau was also like Churchill in that he was a clever politician, adroit in handling others.

Sex-rage individuals make very persuasive speakers. Again we cite Churchill, one of the greatest the English-speaking world has ever produced. His eloquence, his wisdom and his humor are a combination of extraordinary power.

Subtlety is another characteristic of the type. They sense with lightninglike rapidity the inner value of a situation. Their subtle intuitive sense makes them excellent diagnosticians and general practioners. The law also is a profession in which they shine. Their deliberative wills, making them wait to render a decision until all the evidence is in, obviously fit them for judgeships. Generally, they have a great desire for the good, and are incorruptible.

So the vocations and avocations of this type will tend to be in the arts and professions. They are painters; playwrights; writers of stories, like Poe and Hawthorne; actors; producers of plays, movies, and television; singers; instrumental performers. They make powerful ministers and priests, doctors, statesmen. Franklin Roosevelt was this type—creative, humorous, a natural leader. He and Churchill developed a warm friendship because they felt the similarity of their points of view. Similar types are generally sympathetic.

In business, the sex-rage drive produces good executives, born as they are to lead. David Sarnoff, of whom I spoke in the last chapter, is of this type. So, too, is Ben Gurion, who is a natural leader.

The sex-rage type is primarily creative. Nothing hinders

the creativity. It is not as deep a creativity as sex-wonder, but it is interested in, and capable of, more varied expressions. Of the three creative types, it is most general in its field of expression.

In this configuration we find Balzac, Hawthorne, Leonardo da Vinci, Tolstoy, Poe, Secretary of State Dean Rusk, U Thant, of the United Nations, and Jacqueline Kennedy.

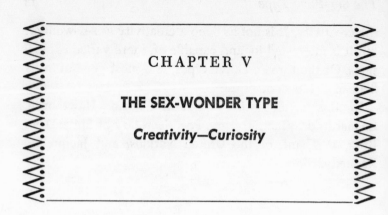

CHAPTER V

THE SEX-WONDER TYPE

Creativity—Curiosity

In the *sex-wonder* type, the creative drive is modified by the drive of curiosity, interpretation. We find here that the drive of creativity is driven deeper by the wonder. Wonder always wants to know the meaning, so the creativity is forced to go deep enough so that the meaning may be discovered. In short, this type goes more deeply into experience than any other. The result is that it usually takes a very long time to find the work in life that will best suit it. The type develops later than all others.

As I said earlier, Lincoln is the outstanding example of the type. He failed at everything he tackled—or at least he didn't achieve success—until he was elected President. As the world sees it, failure after failure was his lot. For the practical jobs in the world, this type is not so gifted as the more earthy classifications. They lean to the world of thought. They are most interested in ideas, the more profound the better. And of course Lincoln's nature was deeply spiritual.

Since the sex-wonder mind is adaptive, always trying to please the other fellow, hating to say *no*, it would hardly seem that Lincoln could be a good lawyer. Lawyers must be able to say *no* without difficulty! But Lincoln was a great humanitarian, primarily interested in the welfare of men and women, and in such a cause he was ever ready to use his creative gifts.

Basically, he was a great artist and statesman. All you have to do is to read his Gettysburg Address to realize that the man was a poet at heart. No man has handled the English language with such genius.

We pick the teacher in all fields as the prototype of the sex-wonder individual. *I understand* is the phrase that most aptly describes him. His whole attention is given to understanding, and then creating.

There is a great difference between the inner nature and the outer behaviour in this type. They are full of intense feeling inside, but can appear the most impersonal of people on the outside. This often gets in their way in intimate human contacts. The other person thinks they are cool and distant, when this is not the case at all. The love letter of a man of this type is quite different from anything you would expect! With their strong philosophical bent, these people are seeking inner meanings which they express even though they might hurt the feelings of those near to them. In seeking the truth of a particular situation they do not realize how their surface reactions might have affected the other person, might even have deceived him or her.

Of all types they are the most stimulated by their inner stream of consciousness, and least stimulated by their environment. But they can be deeply affected by the environment if they don't like it. They are naturally cooperative, so the compromise and competition of the social scene often gets them down. It frequently forces them to lead solitary lives, rather than adjust to society.

In the old days, they used to go West for the life of a lone cowhand or the search for gold or oil. The church has appealed to many. As philosophers, they become interested in solitary speculation, on the meaning of love and truth. That's why some of the greatest thinkers of all time have been in this category.

We see Socrates as a fine example of the depth of the mind. The Socratic method of getting to the truth by questions was his invention. It was taken over by Freud and used in psychoanalysis. In this method, the series of questions becomes a spiral, continually delving deeper and deeper into the mind to find the ultimate truth. When one answer is made, that is questioned, and the answer to that is questioned, and so on. By this method, the subject yields its basic motivation. This is creative questioning motivated by interpretation to find the hidden meaning.

Another example of this type was Emanuel Swedenborg. Certainly his mind was of the greatest profundity. It was scientific in the usual sense of exactitude of reasoning and expression. In his book *Principia* he propounded a nebular hypothesis twenty years before La Place offered his. Swedenborg's book on the brain is still, in my opinion, one of the finest and most exact pictures of the physical brain. He was considered a great scientist in his day.

Then, at the end of his life, which had been a continual search for the physical seat of the soul, he decided it could not be done by physical means. So he then tried for truth by revelation. The last eighteen years of his life were spent in listening for revelation and in vision, which he described in minute detail. His books speak for themselves, showing a search for truth as comprehensive as was ever made by man.

While he did not *discover* the idea of correspondences, which goes back as far as the Hermetic philosophy of the Egyptians, he applied the concept so thoroughly that his name has come to be connected with that doctrine. The latter is that every physical action or event, every physical manifestation, has a spiritual prototype. "As below, so above." You have a physical hunger; you also experience mental and spiritual hungers. You can experience physical pleasures; you can also experience pleasures of the mind and heart.

It is on this principle of correspondences that the Bible is written. And it was Swedenborg who rediscovered the inner meaning of that great Book. In his interpretation, he makes clear that the Bible is always telling us how to use our minds. So it is a vast and comprehensive psychology of the mind and soul of man. This is a perfect example of the type, working in a mind of great genius. Here creativity and interpretation complemented each other in a most consummate fashion.

Seabury, who was this type himself, describes the creative-interpretive type as the wise man and the child. On the intellectual or thinking side of the nature it is profound, while often on the emotional side it is childlike.

William Blake, the great British poet, painter, and engraver, was this type. If you try to read his prophetic books, you might find you need an interpreter. He was certainly trying for the most profound thought. This he attained better, to my way of thinking, in his poetry. Within the literal texture of the words lies the most subtle psychological meaning. Blake has been called the prophet of the present psychological age.

Robert Browning is another of this type who shows the same drive for depth and creative interpretation. While he is not quite as subjective as Blake, his work is filled with intense inner metaphysical meaning.

You can see from the examples given that the type runs to the arts and professions. They are lone wolves, never satisfied unless delving deeply into some aspect of life.

Walt Disney is a modern example of the type. He has spent his life entertaining children. Disneyland is his latest effort in that direction. Only a man of this type would be interested in creating such a monument to children. He is stronger on the childlike side than on the wise man side—and the results are delightful.

The type believes in order, but it is order of the universe, not in the house. Dust around the house doesn't bother them a bit; in fact, they seem to like it. But dust in the mind is something else; they sweep that out as soon as possible.

Sex-wonder people can be jacks-of-all-trades. On the more physical planes, they are fine althletes, fine mechanics, men who are able to tackle and learn how to conquer any kind of job.

They are politic with people because of their adaptive will, and usually get along well in human relations. They want to say *yes* always, they want to please the other person always, they want to help and nurture at all times.

Many of this type never discover their real depths. When this is true, they usually wither on the vine. For they must have their interest aroused, or all is lost. They care more about what they do in life than about the pay for it.

Robert E. Lee was this type. He sat a horse as if he were born to it. He was alert, objective, friendly and outgoing. But behind this mask was the great planning, strategic mind, continually active, but revealed to the public only by some brilliant victory.

The nobility of this man's nature, his great spirituality, was shown in an episode late in his life. He was president of Washington College at a minimum salary, having turned down more lucrative offers. Among them was a fifty thousand dollar job as president of an insurance company. Those who offered the position said it was only for the use of his name. "Don't you think," answered Lee, "that if my name is worth fifty thousand dollars a year, I ought to take good care of it?"

One day a student was sent to him for discipline. During the course of the interview, the student said, "But General, *you failed!*" Lee replied without the least resentment, "I hope that you may be more fortunate than I."

The purpose and meaning of life is always a burning question with sex-wonders. When they have humor, it always has some truth to tell concealed within it, always a purpose.

To sum up, the type naturally seeks the professions. The ministry, medicine, research, psychology, metaphysics, the arts in all branches, philosophy appeal to them. They become mystics like Blake and Swedenborg, teachers like Socrates. The goal of the sex-wonder is the profoundest truth, the deepest aspect of love.

I understand describes this type.

Lewis Carroll, Titian, Queen Elizabeth I, Robert Schuman, and Adlai Stevenson are representative of the sex-wonder type.

CHAPTER VI

THE SEX-FEAR TYPE

Creativity—Caution

Sex is the instinct which has to do with the creation of new life. When sublimated into the mental realm, it is much concerned with human relations. In the case of the *sex-fear* type, the love or creative drive is modified by fear or caution. The conflict this sets up, between love and fear, is apparent in the nature of the type and its action.

The love is pure creativity. The fear is caution, foresight, a looking ahead to see the difficulties in the way of any course of action. So, in a person of this type the caution *inhibits* the pure creative drive. It tends to make him fear its creative expression. Very often the type doesn't seem to be creative. The type is basically creative, but the fear holds back the creativity. On the other hand, the love drive may take over and refuse to listen to the fear. Then the creativity may be expressed, but in a wholly improvident manner. The artist starving in his garret shows love without wisdom. He has inhibited the sense of reality which his fear would give him.

Here is an example of the type from the files of David Seabury. A man came to him many years ago from Montana. He was an apple grower. He was very mixed up about his life, and most unhappy. After a relatively short interview, Seabury realized that he was a creative type. So he suggested that B. study architecture. This was greeted with derision. But after a couple of minutes' thought, B. said, "But I've always thought I'd like sculpture." He admitted later that this had never been a conscious thought, and his saying it surprised him very much. It came out of his unconscious. Well, Seabury advised him to sell his apple farm, go to Paris and study sculpture, and prophesied that in two years he'd be having a one-man show there. B. followed the advice, and Seabury's prophecy came true to the letter. B. became a really great and sensitive sculptor. His specialty was heads of Indians. One reason was the subjective quality of their faces, although that, of course, appealed to his artistic soul. But the sex-fear type generally has a single-minded loyalty to some cause for which it will fight to the finish. B. felt that the Indian had had an impossibly unjust deal from the American government, so he did everything in his power to correct the situation. He talked Indians everywhere and at all times. His friends said that no matter where a conversation with him started, it always ended up with the Indians.

Then came the post-war problems, and his social sense, his feeling for his fellow men, took over and directed his life. He gave up sculpture and devoted every moment of his time to the United World Federalists. He was secretary of the New Mexico chapter, without pay, for seven years. During that time he had no source of income whatever, and lived on the most meager diet. But he carried the torch for the movement wholeheartedly and enthusiastically. He was typical of the iconoclastic side of the type. His letters were full of wit and creative phrases. He expressed a passionate desire to keep mankind from racial suicide. The practical side of the type, which is usually quite common, never appeared in him. He was all love and no practical wisdom.

This type is never lazy. They are continually doing something, and doing it enthusiastically. Their wills are imperative, quick, and decisive, which makes them appear arbitrary. People think they are bossy because their minds work so fast and they are so sure of themselves. But actually, because of the inner conflict between the love and the fear, they are not as confident as they appear.

Their minds are original and creative, and many of the type are extremely witty. What they say is often arresting because of their startling creativity. Their wit is often like a cutting sword, not the humor of the sex-rage type. Used against outmoded ideas, their wit is devastatingly effective. Used personally, in human relations, its results are not conducive to harmony.

These are the people who, like Paul Revere, sound the alarm. They arouse others to the enormity of a situation. They carry the torch with an enthusiasm unmatched by any other type. Intensity is a characteristic of the type. This can seem to be domination, but is not meant to be. The utter earnestness of the mind is what makes it seem so.

When the nature is working as it should, without neurosis, then the fear or caution directs the creativity into the most productive channel possible. Then this nature goes very far, because it sticks to one line.

People of this type are often pioneers in whatever field they choose. William James was such a pioneer in the jungle of the mind. He himself went through a severe nervous breakdown when he was young. There were times when he couldn't find any worth-while meanings in life. It was a spiritual problem with him. During these five years of spiritual battle he worked on all his weaknesses. So, when he came back to life, he had learned to control his imperative will, and hesitated before speaking out. So he presented to the world one of the most charming personalities it is possible to find.

In his book, *Varieties of Religious Experience,* he says this about that period. "In general, I dreaded to be left alone. I remember wondering how other people could live, how I myself had ever lived, so unconscious of that pit of insecurity beneath the surface of life. My mother, in particular, a very cheerful person, seemed to me a perfect paradox in her unconsciousness of danger, which you may well believe I was very careful not to disturb by revelations of my own state of mind. I have always thought that this experience of mine had a religious bearing . . . I mean that the fear was so evasive and powerful, that if I had not clung to the Scriptures . . . texts like *The eternal God is my refuge,* and so forth; *Come unto Me, all ye that labor and are heavy-laden,* and so forth; *I am the resurrection and the life,* etcetera, I think I should have grown really insane."

But this great man pulled himself out of his despondency to become the most eminent psychologist this country has produced. In his James-Lange theory he has made a very creative contribution to the small amount of knowledge man has on the subject of emotion. This theory is that the emotion you feel is produced by your bodily manifestations. You fear because you run. You love because you are drawn to touch the other person. He was a most inspiring teacher at Harvard, and a lecturer as well-known in Europe as in America.

One of the greatest teachers of music, who helped to change the appreciation of music in the United States, was Thomas Whitney Surette, who was this type. He had great wit, could read poetry as few have been able to, and could inspire youth with a burning desire for good music. He taught teachers how to teach music to children. He emphasized the necessity for standards of taste in music, and for that purpose advocated the teaching of folk tunes. Certainly he was an iconoclast in his desire to change the taste in music of the America of his time.

He was the first to give lectures in music appreciation, and for years had the David Mannes Lectureship at the Metropolitan Museum. Walter Damrosch and his orchestra illustrated these lectures.

Due to this man, and also to his friend, Dr. Archibald Davison at Harvard, the singing of school and college glee clubs has been tremendously changed for the better. In the old days they used to perpetrate such songs as "Boola Boola," "March, March on Down the Field," the Cannon Song of Princeton, "There is a Tavern In a Town," ad infinitum. Today the programs of modern college glee clubs contain some of the finest choral music in the world.

Frank Lloyd Wright was another of this type. Whether you like his kind of architecture or not, you will agree that he was an iconoclast, contemptuous of the old and a vociferous advocate of the new—*his* new. He was vastly sure of his opinions, and would purposely ask questions so that he could rebut the answers he got. All the world was his stage, and he was the chief actor. Anyone could see that he had an imperative will, a quick and arbitrary mind.

Lyndon Johnson is a sex-fear type. He is always in a hurry. His imperative will keeps driving him. It is said that often he would dash out of his office with his secretary running down the hall after him to get the last words of a letter he had started dictating before he left. He always expects immediate answers to his questions, and he has his own answers ready instantaneously. He is unusual, for the type, in being felicitous in human relations, and therefore he is able to handle the Senate successfully as its leader. He is witty, and able to find the weak spot in the other person's position.

In business, this type is fine at publicity, at selling— if he is convinced of the worth of the product. He enjoys newspaper work, publishing, drama in all its forms, the ministry, research, medicine. He writes usually to expose some sham or other. He's usually heard, because his voice is so loud.

To summarize, the sex-fear type is a crusader. He wants to help his fellow man, and believes he knows how it should be done. He can and does create in any field. He doesn't like to be bossed, although he does like to boss. The phrase used to describe the type is *I am.*

When the mind is healthy, it is like yeast, permeating the dough of the slothful thinking of man, and rousing it to action.

Other members of this group are Rousseau, Florence Nightingale, Joan of Arc, General De Gaule, Henry Luce.

THE SEX DRIVE

SUMMARY

ACCENT IS ON CREATIVITY AND NURTURE

SENSES TRENDS

ALWAYS WANTS NEW IDEA OR NEW FORM OF EXPRESSION

PIONEER IN THOUGHT AND FEELING

SCHIZOID INTROVERT

EMOTIONAL REACTION INSTANTANEOUS

INTUITIVE REASON

REASONS BY FREE ASSOCIATION

DISLIKES ROUTINE

PREFERS LONE WOLF JOBS

SEX-RAGE

The Leader—*I command*
Deliberative—slow in making decisions
Somewhat aloof—noble
Works on a large scale
Likes familiar surroundings
Strong dramatic sense
Charm, elfish humor
Creative in most ways
Interested in subject rather than object

SEX-FEAR

The Promoter—*I am*
Imperative—Makes quick decisions
Strong convictions
Has sharp corners
Exciting personality
Crusading type
Sharp wit—an idol-breaker
Doesn't seem like love type, but he is
Sensitive to criticism of himself
Often seems like a cycloid

SEX-WONDER

The Teacher—*I understand*
Adaptive will—Makes up mind quickly, but doesn't speak until he knows what other persons wants
Wants to please—hard to say *no*
Slow in finding his place in the world
Completely disinterested in material order
Impersonal
Humor generally has a purpose
Interested in finding the meaning of life
Likes systems of thought

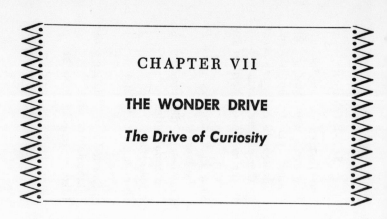

CHAPTER VII

THE WONDER DRIVE

The Drive of Curiosity

The Killian Report gave four cogent reasons for pursuing a course of active space exploration. The first was *curiosity*—the drive that has impelled so much of human progress, when no practical benefits seemed likely to follow.

Carl Gustave Jung, who was one of the foremost psychiatrists, presents a beautiful example of the wonder drive. He was continually questioning, continually searching, seeking for the meaning of life, discovering new aspects of the unconscious. It is heartening to realize that such a scientific mind as his finally came to believe that man has a soul. Where the pseudo-scientific shrink away from the word spiritual, Jung was a strong believer in concepts of God and the Devil. In complete opposition to Freud, he made the statement that the religious instinct is as strong as the sexual, and man can ignore it only at his peril. He was working on a tremendous treatise—three volumes on alchemy. His curiosity was omnivorous, and he felt that in alchemy there is a world of mysterious symbolism which can be used psychologically. Out of his investigations of myths, fairy tales and religious visions, Jung made great discoveries, including that of the race or collective unconscious, the shadowy or dark side of humanity which has engaged so much of his attention. He was continually investigating the dream life, to bring up the problems which are disturbing the unconscious. Out of all this investigation, which was motivated by his wonder drive, Jung came to the following conclusion: "The idea of an all-powerful being is present everywhere. If not consciously recognized, then unconsciously accepted . . . I consider it wiser to recognize the idea of God consciously, otherwise something else becomes God, as a rule, something quite inappropriate and stupid, such as only an 'enlightened' consciousness can devise." (Quoted in *Time* 7/7/52)

Here is another scientist, Dr. Warren Weaver, whose wonder drive has led him to the same conclusions that Jung has reached. After years of scientific investigation in the natural sciences, he comes to this conclusion, "In answering the question, Can a scientist believe in God? I accept two sets of ideas of God, the everyday concept of an emotional and intuitive God, and the intellectual concept of an abstract God, for the very good reason that I find both of them personally satisfying. It does not at all worry me that these are two rather different sets of ideas. Scientists think of electrons as being both (or either) particles and waves. If an electron can be two wholly inconsistent things, it is a little narrow to expect so much less of God. Can a scientist believe in God? I think that God has revealed himself to many at many times and in many places. He continually reveals himself to man today: every new discovery of science is a further 'revelation' of the order which God has built into his universe. I believe that the Bible is the purest revelation we have of the nature and goodness of God." (Quoted in *Look*, 4/5/55)

These are two notable examples of the finest aspect of the wonder drive as it searches continually to find more and more of the hidden meanings of life.

The great drive of wonder stems from the instinct of curiosity. It is a primary emotion. Anyone can see the signs of it in the inquisitiveness of a child. It is the drive by which he learns about his environment, and how to control it. It is continually forcing him to touch things, to look at things, to listen, taste and smell—in other words, to use his senses. The wonder drive is, in essence, the emotional motivator of the later intellect. The child who asks a million questions, who always wants to know why, what, when, how, will be found to have this drive accented in him.

The child hungers to know about his world. This is curiosity. When something happens, he wants to know all the details. Why did it happen? What was it all about? If we didn't have this great instinctive drive, we would be unable to handle the events that are continually happening to us. Wonder has been satisfied so many times in our lives that we are able to handle present experience by what we have learned in the past.

Wonder is deeply imbedded in understanding, and motivates it. How else would the understanding start to function, except under the prodding of wonder?

Wonder is the quality that is most distinct in man as contrasted with the lower animals. For man's wonder can be turned on himself. He is curious about himself and his reactions.

The psychologist uses wonder in his investigations into the meanings of the reactions of the sick mind. The scientist like Einstein wonders about the physical constitution and meaning of the universe. He wonders about light, mass, weight, time, space. Wonder wants to know what man *is*, and starts him on his great and necessary journey to find his true identity. The subject of this book is just that—a search for the meaning of your identity. When you know yourself as you are, this truth, like all truth, will set you free.

Wonder types find the use of their curiosity so fascinating that they sometimes forget all else. They spend so much time in research and inquiry that they become cool, lost in thought and theory. So they often fail to put their discoveries to use. For the same reason they often seem less warm in human relations than other types. They tend to be thinkers rather than doers. Frequently they are not too efficient, because their interest is in the subject rather than in method and procedure.

The animal uses wonder for very simple but necessary aspects of his life. It makes him aware of danger, when his sense of smell gives him the scent of an enemy on the wind. If he had no wonder, he wouldn't protect himself. He uses the instinct to find food, water and shelter. Beyond these, he does not go.

But man uses wonder in its sublimated form for these purposes, and for many others. This is the drive that has made him safe in nature. Can't you see one of our primitive ancestors sitting beside the door of his cave, idly looking at the grass growing beside him? Curious, he pulls a stalk and puts in his mouth. Surprise! It tastes quite good. He takes a stalk to show the woman. From there on, it's not such a great step to the woman's planting a garden, for women were the first gardeners. In this way, as far as we can surmise, began the first cultivation of wheat.

This is curiosity at work. It is the great interpretive drive of wonder applying itself to one aspect of primitive life. Thus did many ideas develop until finally some ancient genius, probably a wonder type, conceived the idea of the wheel and man made one of his greatest strides to power over nature. The basis of modern industrial civilization was laid.

So from one point of awareness to the next, man has progressed ever since. And today this great drive of wonder has unlocked the secret of the atom, discovering cosmic power. Now men and women are wondering whether we have not seized physical power too soon, before we have investigated our own spiritual powers enough to *control* the atomic power we have loosed.

Step by step, hour by hour, year by year, men of this drive have continued their great investigations into the secrets of nature. Today we accept our ease and comfort in nature, rarely thinking of all the wonder that has gone into producing it.

Today the earth has been pretty well explored. Except for parts of the Amazon basin, parts of Africa and Australia, the world is well-known to us. But Admiral Byrd started a new exploration, into the Antarctic. Now that hitherto unknown land is being mapped, and its physical resources investigated. And recently Commander Anderson, in the atomic submarine Nautilus, explored beneath the polar ice cap, travelling from the Pacific to the Atlantic under the North Pole.

Pure research is now a very important subject. On it our very lives may depend. Russia has been doing more research than we, and we realize that we must do more in order to protect ourselves. At present business does a tremendous amount of research. All over the world, in cellars and attics, in research laboratories, men are pursuing their investigations. Some are studying the effect of certain vitamins on animals. And some are trying to produce life itself.

Pavlov was interested in conditioning dogs so that he might discover the facts of the human nervous system. The Russians have used the great man's discoveries to brainwash and torture their victims.

Every month *The Reader's Digest* comes out with the results of someone's investigation of some aspect of life. —How do birds use intelligence? How do bats find their way in the dark? The strange structure of a cow's stomach. The most unforgetable character—the man who is able to arouse curiosity by his life and deeds.

The teacher uses the wonder drive when he explains his subject. The more wonder he arouses in his pupils, the more curiosity, the greater their interest in the subject.

Whenever a man loves a subject, he is curious to know more and more about it. The psychologist is fascinated by the opportunity to learn why the mind acts as it does. He wants to know more and more. Curiosity is the appetite of the mind or intellect. It makes the mind want the food of meaning.

Love is the deepest part of our nature. We don't know very much about it as yet. When we do learn more, it will be wonder that energizes the search. Wonder is the second step in transforming the original love into some form of love on earth.

I watched a man falling in love. I soon saw that wonder was continually at work. First he wondered whether he *was* in love. He decided he was. Then he wondered whether she loved him. Should he ask her now, or later? How much money would he need to get married on? Then he wondered whether he was good enough for her. Was the fact that they had different religious backgrounds a serious matter? At every stage of the courtship, wonder was most active . . . His wonder was trying to make a home for his love.

Think of the wonder in the mind of Columbus as he sailed westward across the unknown ocean. Was his theory correct? Was the world really round? Or would he sail off the edge into space, as his enemies said he would? Columbus was willing to risk death to satisfy his exploring drive.

Think of the wonder of the anthropologist, as he investigates the origins and history of the human race. Every bit of new understanding he obtains adds a little to the fund of information man has about himself, and so adds to his safety in nature.

About two hundred years ago, scientists in Germany and France were trying to find evidences of the great flood described in the Bible. They did a lot of fumbling, turning up artifacts they could not understand. They came to the conclusion that certain prehistoric animals existed long before the advent of man. But then they found the bones of these animals right beside bones of primitive man. At first they were loth to believe the evidence. But finally the proof was so great that they were forced to accept the truth. They discovered that man dated back many thousands of years. This refuted the literal interpretation of the Bible. So, in this case, his wonder led man to a tremendous new concept of truth, the fact that the Bible was not to be read literally.

The wonder drive produces what I call the research mind, the scientific mind in all areas of life. It may appear in the laboratory, like Oppenheimer at Princeton. In Emerson, it showed itself as the scientist of the soul. In Thoreau, it manifested itself in his investigation of nature. Sitting by the shore of Walden Pond, no slightest aspect of nature escaped his intently observing eye.

In Woodrow Wilson we see the scientist-statesman. What was the answer to a world in a continual state of war? His answer, the League of Nations, was the beginning of a solution.

Summing up, wonder is always asking questions and trying to find the answers. What is the meaning behind a certain action? What makes a certain machine act the way it does? What produces certain physical symptoms in the body? What is the method by which these can be relieved?

Wonder is interpretive. It is never satisfied with an apparent fact. It never accepts a statement without question. Wonder wants to know why, but isn't necessarily concerned with curing the problem. It tends to be more interested in the problem per se.

Wonder is the great drive for more light on every subject. It pours the light of meaning on whatever it investigates.

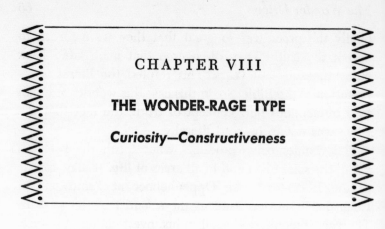

CHAPTER VIII

THE WONDER-RAGE TYPE

Curiosity—Constructiveness

The *wonder-rage* type is most adaptable, most versatile. It is interested in all phases of life, exploring here, investigating there. It is able to give immediate response and understanding. Thus individuals of this type find themselves doing all sorts of jobs that require research and reporting.

The drive of wonder or curiosity is here modified by rage, or the constructive urge, or the mechanical sense. This means that the wonder is driven full steam ahead, with nothing to inhibit it. The result is an omnivorous curiosity that sticks its nose into everything. Nothing is too little or too big for this drive of continual wonder. Because of this quality, the wonder acts horizontally rather than vertically—it spreads all over the landscape, taking in everything. But the rage drives it on and keeps it from going very deep. Therefore these people tend to be interested in many things, never confined to one great interest.

They have adaptive wills, so get along well with others.

However, since they do not like to stick at one thing too long, they do not stick to friendship long enough to really understand the other person. They are more likely to have a number of acquaintances than close friends. Their attention is too easily distracted to other sources of interest.

They are charming, witty and amusing. Exceptional raconteurs, they talk easily and fluently, and are great entertainers. Their descriptions of the many events they have seen are usually enthralling. So the stage appeals to many of them, as does the lecture platform.

One of the great examples of the type is George Bernard Shaw. He was the epitome of wit, and his opinions on every subject under the sun are always fresh and amusing. His plays show an awareness of all the foibles of society. You get the feeling from them that there is no area of life that he has not investigated and formed his opinion on. Every volume of his collected plays contains a preface, a very amusing and wise treatise on life and the theater. He is the born explainer. One of his friends told him that his plays are but explanations.

He was verbal to the highest degree. As a writer he was prolific, and everything he said was done in a completely original way. His wonder was always interpreting, explaining, but freshly and dramatically.

He began his career as a music critic, which is one of the best careers for this type. They can analyze, classify, and criticise with the utmost facility, and what they say usually has a delightful, humorous twist.

Shaw was a deep individual, deeper, perhaps, than most of the type. Under all his bantering, witty persiflage he was a serious person. He knew people, he saw the injustices of the social order, and wanted passionately to make people aware of the shallowness of their thinking. He was the great ironical, satirical critic of his day and age. Here is a bit of Shavian wisdom: "There is only one religion, though there are a hundred versions of it."

Bernard Shaw questioned every idea, and refused ever to take for granted the customs that are accepted by society. Because he questioned so much, he never came up with any solution. One of the best examples of this state of mind occurs in *Man and Superman.* You may remember the episode in hell which Charles Laughton publicized. This had never been played before because it made the play too long. But it was brilliant conversation, with ideas bursting like firecrackers. Yet when it was all over, you had had nothing that could be considered a new contribution to thought. It shows Shaw as the great critic of the social order, the gadfly on the flanks of society.

I have called the *wonder-rage* type the *explorer.* He is the physical explorer who roams all over the earth, examining everything—the way people farm in Patagonia, the latest archeological discoveries in Egypt, and so forth. He is reporting the causes of trouble in the Near and Far East, or the action of the newly-discovered jet streams of polar air which seem to be the primary cause of the weather we experience.

These are reporters, the commentators, writers, publishers, letting the world know the latest events, keeping us all informed about everything that is happening. Their minds can be called encyclopaedic, because of the wealth of factual information they acquire. No matter what question you ask them they will usually be able to supply the most up-to-date answer. Whether it is about some mechanical device, the weather, or the marketing of carnations in New York, they're the ones who can tell you.

While this type *is* interested basically in ideas, because of its continual concern with what is taking place in the world it knows many facts that other wonder types do not.

Joseph Alsop's description of Bertrand Russell shows plainly the physical characteristics of the type. "The room's inhabitant suggests a particularly spry bird. The nose is beak-like; the shock of white hair is a superb crest, and even the voice, high, dry and sometimes a little harsh, is decidedly avian."

Russell is, of course, a very high type. However, he represents the possibilities of the type, just as Shaw does. Let me quote Alsop again, as he summarizes Russell's abilities. "[He] has been a dozen things—great philosopher, great logician, World War I pacifist, World War II anti-Nazi, and always a passionate libertarian and a passionate anti-Communist. But now his life and work are dedicated to a vigorous crusade to ban the nuclear weapons at all costs. Age has not dimmed the power of his mind nor increased his appetite for self-delusion either. What sets Bertrand Russell altogether apart from the vast majority of his fellow-crusaders is mainly his honesty in facing hard facts and hard choices."

Wonder-rage people in general tend to be on the thinking side of life rather than the feeling. They often become intellectuals, immersed in theoretical investigations and somewhat removed from the emotional side of existence. Their wonder about other people and about themselves keeps them from doing the impulsive thing. So they often seem cool and detached in human relations. They feel intensely, but they wonder so much they are never sure about anything—about the feelings of others, or about their own.

This is the type that can become the perpetual student.

He enjoys the questioning attitude so much that he can spend his whole life going from one subject to another.

You will find them in the teaching professions, in all areas. Since they talk well, they easily arouse the interest of others. Thus we are likely to find them not only in teaching as such, but in radio, television, acting, the ministry and the priesthood, in magazine and newspaper work. No routine work for them—they want constant change, work that will continually face them with new aspects.

As they mirror life for you, they generally do not offer the meanings below the surface, although this they can do. But they are at their best when they are giving you their direct, creative responses to the wonders of life and the world.

If they are not emotionally involved, and can be impersonal, they can get at the meaning of an event. They love to play with ideas, and as far as it goes their intuition is amazingly sound. They are stimulated basically by their stream of consciousness rather than by external circumstance, but they generally seem to act on a nice blend of the two.

Almost always brilliant, interesting talkers, fascinating to listen to, they are, like the sex-fear type, arousers of society. They discover the new, and tell the world about it in pleasing ways. They wake up the sleeper. This is a great contribution to life.

The phrase which describes this type is *I perceive.*

We find that Richard Strauss, Elizabeth Barrett Browning, Longfellow, Tennyson and Dante also come within this classification.

CHAPTER IX

THE WONDER-FEAR TYPE

Curiosity—Caution

The *wonder-fear* drive is primarily the drive of interpretation, the drive to discover meaning in all areas of life. It is modified by fear, foresight, caution, and sense perception. This tends to drive the wonder deeper. Unlike the *wonder-rage* type, whose drive is horizontal and wide, the drive of *wonder-fear* is vertical and deep.

The reason why this is so is that the curiosity is held back by the caution from seeing the broad sweep of the scene. The fear makes the curiosity concentrate on what it is looking at until it has exhausted all the possibilities. In *wonder-rage*, the rage drives the curiosity on to ever new fields. In *wonder-fear*, on the other hand, the fear cautions the wonder to get to the bottom of the situation before it turns away its attention.

So we have, in the *wonder-fear* type, the true scientist in the best sense of the term, the scientist in every area of life. And the main tendency of the nature is toward an interest in human relations. Their special genius, their constant, unremitting desire, is to help the underdog, to further amicable race relations, to work for religious freedom, freedom of color, government for the people. The women of the type make felicitous hostesses, always knowing instinctively whom to bring together socially. Wherever the type is, it is always smoothing the rough edges of human relations and helping people to like and understand each other. They are singularly human and sympathetic creatures.

In the field of thought, they interpret and discriminate with much subtlety. Their cautious curiosity is a great asset in dealing with human beings. It gives them judgment and an intuitive vision. They know what to say and when to say it.

Einstein was of this type. Everyone realizes the depth of the man's mind. And everyone knows that he was basically interested in physics, mathematics and pure science. In this field he was a supreme thinker. But the humanitarian side of the type also made its appearance in Einstein. He was more than a pure thinker or a pure dreamer. He was deeply interested in the social aspects of man's life. He gave much thought to the present and future aspects of man's world.

He was always the scientist. He never made a statement without weighing it thoroughly. In the way he went into action, he was deliberative, which is characteristic of the type. He waited until all the evidence was in before he advanced a judgment.

This type gets its stimulation from its own stream of consciousness, and Einstein was no exception. He loved having time to himself, when he could commune with his own thoughts. Here is how he expresses this characteristic: "I live in that solitude that is painful in youth, but delicious in years of maturity."

His democratic quality is shown in this talk on the Negro question. You see here the humanitarian nature coming to the fore. "There is, however, a sombre point in the outlook of Americans. Their sense of equality, of human dignity, is mainly limited to those of white skins. Even among these there are prejudices of which I, as a Jew, am clearly conscious; but they are unimportant in comparison with the attitude of the 'Whites' toward their fellow-citizens of darker complexion, particularly toward Negroes. The more I feel an American, the more the situation pains me. I can escape the feeling of complicity in it only by speaking out."

The great man was deeply interested in human welfare. This is what made him a champion of World Federation as the only means he was able to see for the preservation of the race of man to keep it from exterminating itself through anger and the atomic bomb.

This type produces visionaries who may not be too practical, but nevertheless have their attention fixed on the future safety of the race. Another characteristic is that they don't pay too much attention to the customs and traditions of the day and age. By nature they are pattern-breakers, and attack with vigor what they consider outmoded ideas, customs and manners. Yet even in revolt they are able to retain their mild and gentle natures.

Being a deep type, they are often very subjective. They are interested in principles rather than facts. Some action against a principle they love will fire them to action. They are kind and tender, and often have a flair for the dramatic. They are peace-loving idealists.

The real scientist must be cautious. That is Q.E.D. For anyone can see that an impetuous person, coming to quick conclusions before he had proved his thesis, is no scientist at all. That is why wonder-fear makes the great scientist. His caution is continually telling his wonder, "You'd better work hard on this idea, get to the bottom of it before you try anything else."

The two wise men of Concord, Massachussetts, were both of this type. Emerson was the scientist in the realm of the spirit. Thoreau was the scientist in the realm of nature. There were no trees, animals, birds, or insects that his omnivorous eye did not recognize and pay attention to.

Emerson was what might be called a scientific optimist. He knew the world and the savagery of men. His fear made him cautious in his optimism. He was just as scientific as Einstein, but his attention was not so much on the race of man as upon man's soul. After examining carefully the raw material of the soul, he came at last to the scientific conclusion that man is basically good, not evil. It was a close race man ran with his soul, but the soul wins out as the criterion of man.

Listen to what he says: "Every man is a divinity in disguise, a god playing the fool. It seems as if heaven had sent its insane angels into our world as to an asylum, and here they will break out into their native music and utter at intervals the words they have heard in heaven; then the mad fit returns, and they mope and wallow like dogs." There is the scientist of the soul speaking.

Then the optimist in him speaks: "God is here and now, or nowhere and never," That is the prose of a great man, who is a deep thinker, a mind probing into the secrets of the soul. This is the flash of intuition, the tapping of the stream of consciousness. Emerson is full of these brilliant flashes of cosmic wisdom, like a sudden flash of lightning in the sky.

In his case, the humanitarian characteristic of the type is at its highest intensity. He seeks, and helps men to realize, their essential qualities. Nothing less than the study of the soul itself satisfies him.

His friend Thoreau was different. He was more socially conscious. His article on *Civil Disobedience* was a tremendous influence on Gandhi, and prompted him to use the methods he did in freeing India. He was the man who refused to pay his poll tax and was put in jail. When Emerson came to see him and asked, "Henry, why are you here?" Thoreau's reply was, "Why are you not?"

Thoreau has had a great influence on thinking in America. He appeals to the intellectual critics of the social scene.

Walden was a pioneering work, a satire on the false values of the New England countryside. In it was a critique, biting and still pertinent, of the average man. Thoreau said that he manufactures extraordinary loads of paraphernalia for himself, and then carries this enormous load on his bent back for the rest of his life.

This is how the pithy social comment reads: "I see young men, my townsmen, whose misfortune it is to have inherited farms, houses, barns, cattle and farming tools; for these are more easily acquired than got rid of. . . . They have got to live a man's life, pushing all these things before them, and get on as well as they can. How many a poor immortal soul have I met, well-nigh crushed and smothered under its load, creeping down the road of life, pushing before it a barn seventy-five by forty, and so forth."

You can see that Thoreau belongs to the pattern-breakers. He had a vision of life that he wanted to give to others. He believed that many so-called luxuries of life were real hindrances to a man's development. He said that the wisest of men have always lived in the simplest fashion. This is true, but it is not a truth that the world desires to know.

Coupled with his social satire, was the scientific poet-naturalist, describing the river, the phases of nature, the flora and fauna of his loved region.

To recapitulate, the *wonder-fear* is the great human relational type. Practically every one of them is felicitous in his relations with other people. They are always for the underdog, and in the forefront of every effort to bring peace and fair play into human relationships.

I adjust is the phrase descriptive of this type.

We find that Wordsworth, Yeats and Robert Louis Stevenson are in this grouping.

CHAPTER X

THE WONDER-SEX TYPE

Curiosity—Creativity

The accent of the *wonder-sex* type is artistic. The wonder or interpretive drive is modified by sex or creativity. So the creativity drives on the curiosity. The result of this is that the creative urge enters the interpretation, so whatever is seen is examined creatively. This means a constant interest in new ways of interpretation. This is not the explorer or the scientist, but the architect, who builds for beauty or use in all areas of life.

This makes for a very beautiful nature. Love is behind the curiosity, so the type never shows any but harmonious reactions. It has great perception, amazing adaptability, and a sympathy that makes for lasting and deep personal relations. As mates, the type is felicitous. The guiding principle of both men and women can be said to be, "Whither thou goest, I will go."

The type almost always has good taste, and in some cases it is exquisite. Their sense of harmony demands that they have peace around them at all times. They suffer a lapse in conduct of another with good grace. You will find that even if you have been difficult, they are still ready to cooperate with you.

Their will is imperative, which means that they are quick to make up their minds, and quick to tell you their reactions on any matter. You can, however, disagree with them and they will take your views amicably. The love driving the wonder makes them think of the other person with nurture, and always want to arrive at a state of agreement. There is nothing they hate so much as altercation, for deep within them is an intense desire for harmony, rhythm and balance. This is what gives them their aesthetic drive.

They cannot stand injustice of any kind, either to themselves or to others. They lean over backwards to defend someone whom they believe to be unjustly treated or accused. They do not jump into the world scene as quickly as the wonder-fear types, but in matters of individual justice none are their equals.

Woodrow Wilson was of this type. Of course he was a world figure of heroic proportions. When he was president of Princeton, he developed many plans for the betterment of education there. Among these was the preceptor system, which has now been adopted by other colleges. He considered the club system at Princeton undemocratic. One of his plans was to substitute for it the Quad system, such as is followed at Oxford. This project developed into a great battle, for the old grads liked the clubs.

One night Wilson accepted an invitation to dinner at one of the clubs. A former president of the university, Dr. Patton, who was quite a wit, was also to speak. He was the first speaker, and attacked Wilson's Quad proposal, making many clever Bible quotations to prove his points. He was roundly applauded. The club members wondered what Wilson could possibly say in reply.

Well, he was more than equal to the occasion. He countered all Patton's arguments with very apt Bible phrases. It was such a spontaneous tour de force that when he finished the club members were on their feet cheering him.

He always dressed with great care. In this he showed his sense of harmony, rhythm, and balance so character-istic of the type. But what made his mind really come alive was the principle of harmony, rhythm, and balance in human society. The freedom of the slave, the political and economic slave, the brotherhood of man, all men living together in harmony on this planet—this to him was beauty. All his love went into it. No man in history ever fought more passionately for human welfare than this great figure.

He was one of the greatest speakers of all time. After he had been governor of New Jersey for a short time, and had wrestled with the dirty politics of the bosses, his smooth academic speech found the feeling it had lacked. And ever after, his deep feeling and his creative words made his speeches the equal of those of any public man this country has produced.

He was completely convincing. First, all knew that he believed passionately in what he was saying. He wrote most of his own speeches. Then everyone knew that he was a loving and wise man. The result was that he became first the voice of America, then the voice of the whole world.

His mind was quick and imperative. This made him come to conclusions more rapidly than some approved of.

And his imperative will gave him some trouble in human relations. He was usually sure he was right. This is illustrated by what he said about statesmanship. "Examine every problem carefully, make up your mind, and turn the key."

The type has a one-track mind, and so did Wilson. His attention, once given to a subject, saw nothing else around that center. To him, his ideas were so obviously for human welfare that he could never understand why he got so much opposition.

He was an outstanding example of the sureness and quickness of the type. He was utterly convinced that the League of Nations was the next step for the world to take. He believed that it would solve the problems of nationalism, and competition between nations.

There are not too many of this type who are tough enough to stand the gaff of the world stage. Wilson himself, when the going got rough, succumbed to a stroke and literally gave his life for his dream. The ordeal through which the Senate put him undoubtedly caused his breakdown.

His single-track mind refused to compromise with Lodge and the Senate leaders. He lost his great fight for humanity but he made an inestimable gift to the world. He turned the attention of all men to his great plan, in which he believed freedom for all men lay.

He got great criticism for saying that "America is too proud to fight." But in this creative phrase, which is now accepted by all thinking men, he put the epitome of his type's desire. All sense, all harmony, rhythm, and balance, are lost when men begin to fight.

Because both wonder and sex are subjective, and receive their stimulation from their stream of consciousness, the type is not usually as well-oriented to the facts and objects and circumstances of ordinary life as are the other two wonder types. But give them ideas and principles to work on, and they come alive immediately.

The painter Whistler was a man of this type, sensitive and subtle. There is a mystic, inner stream-of-consciousness quality about his Battersea Bridge that makes it great. Beautifully placed on the canvas, it has a great sense of balance, space, light, and proporation which add to the symmetry of the design.

Then in his famous picture of his mother, we see again the same occult balance and sensitive placing of the figure. It is the idealized picture of all mothers, delicate, shrouded in a mystic feeling-tone. If a mother-complex is ever a good thing, it was in this case.

People of this type make good lawyers, because they love to argue. They love to balance judgments. Each is usually sure that he is right and the other man wrong, a necessary state of mind for a lawyer. But they see both sides of a question, and would never take a side in which they did not believe.

With the accent of the type on beauty and artistic sensitivity, it finds happiness in careers that give those qualities a chance for expression. They are successful in the dance, drama, moving pictures, television, writing, architecture, sculpture, interior decorating, landscape gardening, jewelry, costume design, and so forth.

This type is creative as well as interpretive. It is not so deeply or generally interested in human affairs as in beauty. In human relations, it is best in the intimate union of marriage, or with a few friends. It hasn't generally the great social urge of wonder-fear.

But this type is the builder of beauty everywhere. A gentle, peaceful nature of much inner beauty, it seeks for the harmony of order everywhere. The Greeks recognized that the internal beauty extended to the external beauty. Their statue of Apollo Belvedere has taken this type as its model.

I balance is the phrase used to describe the type.

Daudet, Isadora Duncan, Thomas Hardy, and Mme. Recamier were wonder-sex types.

THE WONDER DRIVE

SUMMARY

ACCENT IS ON INTERPRETATION

ALWAYS WANTS TO KNOW HOW? WHY? WHAT? WHEN?

CURIOSITY—THE GREAT DRIVE FOR MEANING

FIRST STEP IN TAMING NATURE

SCHIZOID EXTRAVERT

EMOTIONAL REACTIONS INSTANTANEOUS

INTUITIVE REASON

FREE ASSOCIATION

DISLIKES ROUTINE

PREFERS LONE-WOLF JOBS

WONDER-RAGE

The Explorer—I investigate
Adaptive will—goes with other person
Interest wide rather than deep
Knows something about everything
On thinking side of life, often intellectual
Cool, impersonal, somewhat brittle
Hosts of friends, few intimates
Brilliant, stimulating—rouses to new ideas
Critic
Reporter
Commentator

WONDER-FEAR

The Scientist in all areas of life—I perceive
Deliberative will—slow in making decisions
Interest deep rather than broad
Perpetual student—never gets to the end of anything
Charming, delightful to be with
Impersonal, but somewhat warmer than wonder-rage
Interested in human relations and social problems
Brother to all men

WONDER-SEX

The Architect—I balance
Imperative—quick decisions
One-track mind
Beauty essential
Wants harmony in all areas—harmony, rhythm and balance his watchword
Sees both sides of question, if emotions are not involved
Somewhat off the earth
Goes with partner, when convinced of the reality of the love relation
Quickness of mind often causes difficulty in human relations

CHAPTER XI

THE RAGE DRIVE

Constructive—Mechanical—Executive

Your mind is the powerhouse of your organism. In it your emotions and thoughts originate in consciousness. You are a combination of feeling and thought united. The power is always the emotion. The way it goes into action is the thought.

We take up here the emotion of *rage*, the constructive or mechanical sense. *Rage* is basically the desire to change things. It is an emotion that wants to get out and build, to affect its environment in some active way. It desires to work with the actual wood or metal, or paper or cloth. *Rage* will take the blueprint of a machine, for instance. It will immediately go to work to find the material for the finished product. Then it will prepare and fit the parts and build the actual machine.

Rage is an emotion of action, not so much of thought and feeling as the creative and interpretive drives are. It is interested in the object and the fact, the material things to be used. It is strong on method and procedure, or how to get the blueprint or design into concrete form.

It weighs the material, judges the speed, and estimates the actual time and space. It handles all aspects of the objective, physical world of three dimensions in which we live.

Also the constructive drive is interested in order. What intelligence does is to establish order where there was chaos before. This is the active intent of the rage drive. It grows our food for us, builds our houses, roads, bridges, airplanes, automobiles, radios, television. It constructs all the many varied, necessary and unnecessary objects and gadgets that we think will make us secure in nature.

The original idea may have come from the creative drive. The wonder drive took that idea and put it into the form of a plan or blueprint. It explained the idea. Now it is in the hands of the builder who makes the idea become the thing.

So man, in his capacity of hand, eyes, tongue, foot, and brain of his Creator, sets out to manufacture the finished article. And his creativity here on the plane of matter is just as ingenious as was the original idea.

So we see the mechanical urge set to do its part. The man with the rage drive has his prodigious cranes, bulldozers, cement mixers, earth-movers. He has his vast steel furnaces, his railroads spanning the country, his mining and oil machinery (which now goes to sea), his great steamers. And then we see him at work on missiles, making gigantic preparations for war, constructing jet planes and intricate farm machinery.

It is an awe-inspiring sight to see how this man has changed the face of nature. And now he has capped all this constructive work as we see the mechanical brain of the great computing machines of IBM.

New York City is a beautiful example of this mechanical genius at work. The streets are filled with automobiles, the buildings are going up to the sky in all directions, while the subways are moaning and groaning below as they carry their millions to work or play. In the rivers tugs are hauling food and oil and pushing great liners into their piers. All this is rage or human energy at work, pulling, hauling, shoving the earth about, pushing the steel and aluminum and glass into the skies.

Now, if you watch any baby you will see that, almost from birth, he fights against restraint of any kind. If you hold him in your arms he begins to wiggle right away. He is telling you without words that he wants to live his life in his own way. This is the instinct of aggression at work. The baby wants to find his own way of life and no one is to stop him. Anything that appears to interfere with his ease is resisted.

When the baby grows up, this drive becomes the aggressive drive of man to free himself from the restraints of nature. It creates the ways and means, the methods and procedures by which man accomplishes this purpose. The drive of rage has also been the means of man's protecting himself from his enemies. He will resist others just as he does nature.

The Hungarian Revolution against the awful tyranny of the Kremlin has been an outstanding example of the action of rage, as it should be used. It is righteous wrath. The whole people went out aggressively to change an intolerable situation. Rage always wants to change things for the better.

First there was the stage of feeling and thought about the pressures of the Kremlin. At that time the idea of rebellion formed in the minds of Hungarian patriots. And through these leaders the people began to understand the monumental injustice of the Russian domination.

The feeling and thought stage finally reached the stage of rage or action. This was the active part, the doing of the job. After the subjective preparation, rage takes over.

Rage is doing. The man or woman with that accent is a doer. Rage says, "Let's quit thinking about it and get into action. Let's put this idea into form, think of actual steps to take, action that will be most efficient. Let's design the tools necessary to build the object we have in mind."

And so the earth is moved, the road or bridge is built, the building is fabricated, the chemical processes are changed, improved and refined, the physical properties of matter are handled by continually new methods. Week by week new methods and processes are discovered by this great drive.

Before you can become used to one method you are offered another. We used to go into a grocery store and be served by clerks. Now the method and procedure has been changed to self-service, in the new supermarket. Even the place and style of the shelf dispensing tomato cans may be changed at any moment.

In the construction of the great machines of America all drives were necessary. But it was the drive of rage that did a lot of the actual hammering and sawing.

There are more famous men in the rage category than in any other. For what the rage drive does in its handling of matter is so apparent that it gets immediate recognition. You are able to see the building rise in the air, or the road being completed for traffic.

Executive capacity is a rage characteristic. The organization of great industrial plants is largely in the hands of this type. Office managers and superintendents of plants are often of this drive.

The rage drive likes others and is therefore popular. They can both give and take orders and like it. They are willing to take routine jobs and carry on for long hours at a stretch.

Most representative of the rage drive as a whole is the engineer in all fields. One man shovels the earth around, another builds the electronic wonders of radio, television, radar, and the thinking machines. The efficiency engineer tells how to improve the methods and processes of the plant to which he is called. Other engineers, too numerous to put down here, are working in the atomic field on missiles, on engines for submarines, on countless industrial processes.

Rage types tend to be orderly and systematic. They will work out ingenious card index systems, new methods of filing. They like the order imposed by machinery. The pilot of a jet plane thrives on the demand made on his ingenuity by the complicated machine. Watch the face of a rage type light up as he raises the hood of a new car and sees the beauty of the engine.

Action, energy, doing something concrete, makes these individuals come alive. With their love for people they are continually joining organizations. They are the church workers, they join hospital drives, they offer to do town work. They love college associations, political parties, clubs. They are the typical joiners.

They work in the Scout movements, the YMCA. They like to talk and argue. But this talk is usually about facts, objects, happenings, methods, and procedures, not about ideas. These the ordinary man of the type leaves strictly alone.

There are many famous bankers in this category. They are the men who like to hold what they have made. Their judgment on fiscal matters is good. It is not without reason that the big businessman or the banker is often caricatured as a big, powerful, round-headed man.

On a high plane we see such a man as Washington as a representative of the type. A leader of men, of the utmost probity, a great soldier, he typifies the rage type at its best. And Franklin also, equally great, was this drive. And he, of course, added to all his marvellous wisdom, was one of the great scientists of all time. Electricity was not the same after Franklin.

Rage is the fighting quality of man and stems from the instinct of pugnacity. Without its use man would not be where he is today. It has been a necessary weapon in the defence of civilization through the ages.

The rage drive does a tremendous amount of work. It seems to do more than other types because what it does can be seen with the naked eye.

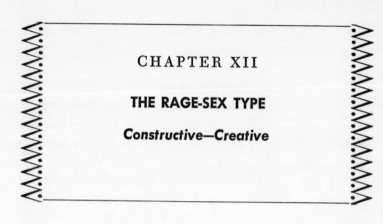

CHAPTER XII

THE RAGE-SEX TYPE

Constructive—Creative

I am going to begin the description of this type by quoting Thomas Jefferson as he describes Washington, who was a *rage-sex* type. He gives an almost complete rounding out of the qualities of the type. Here are his words in part:

"I think I knew Gen. Washington intimately and thoroughly. His mind was great and powerful, without being of the very first order; his penetration strong, though not so acute as a Newton, Bacon or Locke; and as far as he saw, no judgment was ever sounder. It was slow in operation, being little aided by invention or imagination, but sure in conclusion. Hence the common remark of his officers of the advantage he derived from councils of war, where, hearing all suggestions, he selected whatever was best; and certainly no general ever planned his battles more judicially. But if deranged during the course of the action, if any member of his plan was dislocated by sudden circumstances, he was slow in readjustment. He was incapable of fear, meeting personal dangers with the calmest unconcern. Perhaps the strongest feature in his character was prudence, never acting until every circumstance, every consideration was maturely weighed, refraining if he was in doubt, but when once decided going through with his purpose whatever obstacles opposed. His integrity was most pure, his justice the most inflexible I have ever known; no motives of interest or consanguinity of friendship or hatred being able to bias his decision. He was indeed in every sense of the word a wise, a good and a great man. His temper was naturally high-toned; but reflection and resolution had obtained a firm and habitual ascendance over it. If, however, it broke its bonds, he was most tremendous in his wrath. In his expenses he was honorable but exact; liberal in contributions to whatever promised utility; but frowning and unyielding on all visionary projects and all unworthy calls on his charity. His heart was not warm in its affections; but he exactly calculated every man's value, and gave him a solid esteem proportioned to it. Although in the circle of his friends where he might be unreserved with safety, he took a free share in conversation, his colloquial talents were not above mediocrity, possessing neither copiousness of ideas nor fluency of words. In public, when called on for a sudden opinion, he was unready, short and embarrassed. Yet he wrote readily rather diffusely in an easy and correct style. He was naturally distrustful of men, and was inclined to gloomy apprehensions; and I was ever persuaded that a belief that we must at length end in something like the British Constitution had some weight in his adoption of the ceremonies of levees, birthdays, pompous meetings with Congress, and other forms of the same character, calculated to prepare us gradually for a change which he believed possible, and to let it come on with as little shock as might be to the public mind. On the whole his character was in its mass perfect, in nothing bad, in few points indifferent, and it may truly be said that never did nature and fortune combine to make a man great and to place him in the same constellation with whatever worthies have merited from man an everlasting remembrance."

Now that is a very wonderful description of an individual rage-sex type of genius. But all the characteristics described in this penetrating analysis can be found in lesser degree in people of the same type with less endowment.

Benjamin Franklin was also of this type. While the usual humor of the type is broad and somewhat clownish, this was not true in his case. For in Franklin there flowed a fresh and crystal stream of inimitable humor. This poured from the springs of the earth wisdom he was full of. Poor Richard's Almanac was a mine of homely practical wisdom couched in humorous terms. Some of his phrases have become immortal.

At the meeting of the Second Continental Congress gathered to ratify the Declaration of Independence, Jefferson, its author, was sitting next to Franklin. As the criticism of the members went on, and paragraph after paragraph was expunged, Franklin could see that Jefferson was not enjoying watching his child being cut up.

To relieve the situation he told Jefferson the following story: "I have made it a rule, whenever in my power, to avoid becoming the draughtsman of papers to be reviewed by a public body. I took my lesson from an incident which I will relate to you.

"When I was a journeyman printer, one of my companions, having served out his time as apprentice hatter, was about to open shop for himself. His first concern was to have a handsome signboard with the proper inscription.

"He composed it in these words: JOHN THOMPSON, HATTER, MAKES AND SELLS HATS FOR READY MONEY, with the figure of a hat subjoined.

"But he thought he would submit it to his friends for amendments. The first he showed it to thought the word HATTER tautologous because followed by the words, MAKES HATS. If good and to their liking they would buy by whomsoever made. It was struck out.

"The next observed that the word MAKES might as well be omitted, because his customers would not care who made the hats. If good and to their liking they would buy by whomsoever made.

"A third said he thought the words FOR READY MONEY were useless as it was not the custom of the place to sell on credit. Everyone who purchased expected to pay. They were parted with and the inscription now stood JOHN THOMPSON, SELLS HATS.

" 'Sells hats!' says his next friend. 'Why nobody will expect you to give them away. What then is the use of that word?' It was stricken out. And HATS followed it, the rather as there was one painted on the board. So the inscription was reduced ultimately to JOHN THOMPSON with the figure of a hat subjoined."

When we take the mind apart and talk about it in its different aspects, we do this because we can only explain it this way. So as we talk about the rage-sex drive, please do not get the idea that it is motivated exclusively by rage. The same mind has within it creativity, interpretation, sense perception. It is only that the rage part of the mind is accented. And so when the rage-sex type uses its creativity it does so in a constructive, mechanical way.

In the rage-sex drive we find a tremendous amount of energy. The constructive, building drive is modified by sex or creativity. This means that great power is developed because the creativity drives on the original constructive sense, not inhibiting it at all.

Seabury calls this type a courage-love nature. In the finest of the type there is great fortitude, analytic and constructive vision, deep feeling for the fellow man. These are very solid individuals. When they have problems they can be a little heavy. They are loyal and can always be depended upon. They can be very tenacious, holding on to a dull job with great determination.

They are like bulls or bulldogs, and are tough men in a fight. All those who met Jack Dempsey can testify to this quality. They are aggressive, and "Common Sense" is the flag they carry at their masthead. And so they tend to be conservative and are likely to dislike all theoretical ideas. They are always interested in the object and the fact, in the controlled test, the logical approach, the proven statement. *I have* is the phrase which describes them most accurately. They like possessions and get them and hold them.

This type is literally the one which moves mountains, and so we pick the engineer as illustrative of the drive. Often they become contractors whose great earth-moving machinery, bulldozers, road-laying equipment and cement mixers we see all over the landscape. These people like bigness and weight, and nothing physical frightens them.

They are the farmers who get up at four in the morning

and work hard all day. They can do a prodigious amount of physical labor, handling their farm machinery with skill.

On other planes of life they are bankers, who can make and hold on to money for themselves and others. In the last decade, the time of the money barons, they often became captains of industry. They were prominent in the push of civilization to the west coast in that era.

They are competitive and like to test their strength against that of others. But in the highest sense this characteristic is really the desire to perfect the self so as to serve others better.

A man of this type, who recently rose to the top, is Charles E. Wilson. He was for many years head of General Motors and then became Secretary of Defense under Eisenhower. He is a man of facts and figures with no particular interest in theory. His imagination is only related to facts and objects. He likes the logical approach, the controlled test, and tends to judge the future by the past.

The rage-sex type is big in all areas, big in body, big in idea, big in accomplishment. The mind is slow to come to a decision but when that decision is made, it is held to with great obstinacy.

It is very interesting to see that Jefferson noted this characteristic in Washington. What it means is that the type has a deliberative will, and waits till all the evidence is in before making up its mind.

No one can push these people out of their chosen course of action. General Grant was a man of this type and admirably displayed its aggressive qualities. He was not a brilliant strategist, but his statement "I propose to fight it out on this line if it takes all summer" is illustrative of the rage-sex characteristic of determination.

I have is the phrase used to describe the type.

Immanuel Kant, Mark Twain, Hogarth, Rabelais, Caruso, and General Grant are among those in this grouping.

CHAPTER XIII

THE RAGE-WONDER TYPE

Constructive—Interpretive

In this type the drive for mechanics, construction, and executive sense is modified by wonder or curiosity, the interpretive drive. This qualifies the energy of the rage and drives it deeper into whatever course it decides to follow. In doing this it seems to inculcate into the type a most extraordinary working habit and ability. These are the people who are forever at work. And they accomplish a prodigious amount from their incessant effort.

Because the wonder drives the mind deep into a subject, you will find many great scientists like Michael Faraday and Charles Darwin in this grouping.

Faraday was a great genius, and genius always transcends all type classifications. But he illustrates the best qualities of the drive very well. He was the great analyser, realistic, accurate. His creative sense of interpretation was always focussed on looking for the new. Through his tremendous determination and indefatigable work he was finally led to discover how to harness the source of electricity. He is responsible for the basic power which has so many uses for us today in the home and in industry and transportation.

Strangely enough, he was not interested in making money. For usually the rage types have a well-developed money sense. But he was vitally interested in finding out the secrets of nature. And this interest led him continually on to many other discoveries that satisfied his nature. So he gave up voluntarily the fortune he could have made from his great discovery.

In another way Faraday also contradicted the usual bent of the drive. They are usually anything but great lovers. But Faraday married a wife with whom he was extremely compatible. So compatible that she agreed with his decision not to go all out for a fortune. Theirs was a perfect mating.

The *rage-wonder* type is very loyal. They make the most faithful of mates and friends. Charles Darwin was another fine example of the type. Again, as in the case of Faraday, we see the most meticulous accuracy. We witness the gaze that penetrated deeper into nature than man had ever gone before. Again there was exhibited the great power of analysis, the complete dedication to the scientific attitude.

This is the man who started out in life to be a minister, who lived to throw organized religion into the greatest turmoil it had ever experienced. For the religious of that day said that Darwin had banished God from heaven.

But the great man, whose *The Origin of Species* changed the thought of mankind, went on his way inexorably, aiming to find and tell the truth at all costs. "Facts, facts, I must have proof," said Darwin. And in this sentence was compressed his attitude toward life. Twenty years of that life were spent in the gathering of the these facts on the Galapagos.

When it appeared that his whole life work was to be stolen from him by the paper of Alfred Russel Wallace, he did all he could to help Wallace. Probity, honor were always carried at his masthead. The truth was a sacred obligation. He was a genius and a big mind. There was nothing petty about him. He said of those who attacked his revolutionary ideas, "Let each man hope and believe what he can."

Darwin and Faraday were world-shaking figures. The careful, precise nature of their minds demanded the deepest possible search for truth. And both were rewarded by their investigations into the secrets of nature.

Sir Joshua Reynolds was a painter of this type. He was realistic, a wonderfully careful technician. He gave you the exact representation of the person or scene he was painting. There was nothing abstract about his work. It was concise, true to life and to nature. No mysticism bothered him. He was not searching for inner meanings. He was out to express the external beauty of what he saw.

The *rage-wonder* type is par excellence the careful observer of detail that others pass over, of the truth of nature and the ways of men. They tend to be restrained in human relations. They seldom appear over-emotional. In business they exhibit a shrewd, wary judgment in affairs. This ability, coupled with the fact of their loyalty, makes them fit for positions of trust in the business world. Their capacity for statistics makes them very useful in the banking business. They become the expert accountants, the treasurers, the confidential secretaries, where their natural abilities fit very nicely.

The type is adaptive. It will go with you easily. It is intent on pleasing the other person. But it keeps its secrets well. You may know a *rage-wonder* type for a long time but never get to his deeper regions of mind. They sometimes have a hard time finding out their inner thoughts for themselves.

The type lives in relation to its setting. Their environments tend to be books, scientific laboratories, mechanics' benches, the secretarial desk. Or they seek the stretches of nature, fields, woods, mountains, streams, and sea. They are affected by these more than by human beings.

They do not need human contacts as much as the other cycloids do. They tend to analyze people, to criticise them, and finally arrive at some intellectual decision about them. This may be just, and does not err on the warm and friendly side.

The criticalness of Voltaire illustrates how meticulous the type is in letters. He was discriminating to a pronounced degree. He possessed a shrewd, apprehensive judgment. Nothing in the foibles and errors of society escaped his microscopic mind. But he needed the stimulus of the society in which he lived for the inspiration of his writing.

The people of this group often show great acumen. They sometimes tend to become great intellects. They do not like to let their feelings out to play. Often they can be bogged down in detail.

Agassiz, the naturalist, was this type. In watching nature, his quality of attention to detail was a great asset. And like Darwin, Agassiz penetrated deep into nature.

Then, on the more mechanical plane, the constructive plane, this type shows special aptitudes. During the last war I picked up a copy of *Life* magazine. I glanced at a page where there were displayed the faces of about twenty-four aces of the air war. I was astonished as I saw the faces side by side. For each man looked as if he were the brother of the man next to him. I remember talking to Seabury about this. He said, "Well, the answer is that they are all rage-wonder types. These are the best of all types in handling machines in motion."

The type make very fine mechanics, especially where attention to detail is important. And when it comes to judging speeds, distances, directions, proximity there is no drive so good. So they will be found in all types of transportation, on the roads, in the air, on the rails, under the sea.

The quality of being aware of their surroundings is a mark of this type. They do not tend to have accidents, because they see everything around them. And they see these things in relation to each other and to them. They therefore take any precautions necessary.

They make good teachers, particularly in science, where their accuracy and scientific approach are most important. They are good in history, anthropology, biology, physics, the subjects where knowledge of detail is necessary.

I analyze is the term that describes the type and its action. They, like all rage types, desire to change things, and not just on the surface, either. They analyze before they attempt to change. So what they do usually has a lasting quality.

The term mechanic fits the general run of the type. They construct and build. They are strong at method and procedure and process, for their analytical minds give them the method that is most efficient. Even Faraday

showed great mechanical sense as he worked in his laboratory.

Constant energy, meticulous observation, scientific
know-how—these are the great abilities of the type. In
the genius this makes a tremendous impact on life.

Dickens, Copernicus, Andrew Carnegie, Calvin Cool-
idge and Sir Joshua Reynolds come under this classification.

CHAPTER XIV

THE RAGE-FEAR TYPE

Constructive—Cautious

It is possible to speak of the *rage-fear* configuration as a courage-caution combination. For we have here rage or energy, constructive sense, and mechanical ability modified by the drive of fear, caution, foresight, and sense perception. The caution tends to slow down the energy, often causing it to go deeper than in the other two rage types. The energy is throttled down by the caution, but this fact drives it to more subjective expression when the type is a high one. And the caution can drive the energy underground.

This type is capable of great depths and heights of feeling and thought. So that wherever they are you are aware of them at all times. The fear may seem to stop the energy, but you feel that the potential is always there.

Seabury has this interesting statement to make of the effect of the modifier on the primary drive. He says, "It is the secondary emotion that gives the *formative* expression to the configuration, because it affects the way a person acts rather than how he feels." So in this case the fear dictates to the rage how it shall act.

This is therefore a very self-controlled type. It can become inhibited on account of its caution, while inside the energy boils around trying to find some constructive outlet.

Seabury states that in the higher planes of this type there is a beautiful capacity to endure privation for the fulfillment of a great purpose or ideal. Some of the religious martyrs have belonged to this grouping, for none is more able to sacrifice than those whose courage is balanced by caution.

It would seem that the fear drives the energy to seek the ideal of perfection that lies within each one of us. What this does in the *rage-fear* type is to make them very ambitious. There is within them an intense desire for success and its subsidiary, a strong drive for power.

There is nothing wrong with this drive to make the self the very best instrument of life possible. In fact, it is a very positive quality. It is only when the drive is for one's own aggrandisement that the power drive gets out of hand and becomes negative.

Interestingly enough, most of the type are mountain climbers desirous of attaining the highest spot within reach. It seems to express to them in terms that are acceptable the perfection within them that they are always trying to release. After all, when you have climbed with great effort to the top of a 10,000 foot peak, you have for the time achieved perfection. No one in your locality can do any better. Standing on the summit of a mountain symbolizes reaching the top in other areas.

There is a certain amount of inner conflict in this mind.

It is between feeling and thought. Usually the thought wins out and controls the behavior pattern. When, however, the feeling and thought are not in conflict but united you have an individual of extraordinary generosity and power. This occurs only in the higher types.

Many of this type make fine lawyers. Their minds are extremely quick and agile. *I manoeuvre* is the phrase that best describes the way their minds work. The famous Machiavelli was of this type and gave his name to the skillful manoeuvring of the mind. He illustrates, not too positively the extraordinary cleverness of the type. In his book, *The Prince,* he describes how the prince can seize and wield his power. Unfortunately he makes use of all the forms of fear to do this. These are many and devious. That is why his name has come to stand for the clever and unscrupulous use of power for its own sake. For he advised all the chicanery and deceit that go with such use of fear.

Harry Truman is a good example of the type on the plane of common sense and the political life. He is no Machiavelli, let me hasten to add. He is an honest man of unusual ability, who shows great interest in and capacity for politics. He likes people perhaps more than the average of the type does. He has the quick, decisive mind of this drive. You always get an immediate answer from him on any subject. This betrays the imperative will of the type. They think fast and know immediately what they think on all subjects.

Truman had no general overall policy to guide his administration. He was not a planner like Woodrow Wilson, for instance. He was a realist, a doer, not a thinker. But he was able to make quick and wise decisions in a crisis. This he proved by his great decision to go into Korea, by which he saved that country from Communist domination. This type of mind is fine in a crisis where quick decision has to be made on the spot.

Since these minds are imperative, they usually have to learn to curb this tendency, for they find that they do have trouble in human relations. Most of them do this in early life. But this was not exactly true of Truman. As we well remember he could suddenly become explosive, and did, on the subject of Margaret.

The average members of the type like to work for big companies. There seems to be something about the bigness that satisfies their inner drive for perfection. Many are born officials, loving to rule, yet fearing it. Remarkably industrious, they are great students, academic searchers for knowledge. Many of them are teachers and college professors. The government, being large, appeals to their sense of prestige. You will find many of them in bureaucratic positions. They are also mechanical and are found wherever there are machines.

This type is the engineer who likes to handle the most intricate machinery, the electronic engineer rather than the man who runs a Diesel.

Delicate manoeuvring with hand and brain please this disposition. It is the near perfection of the more elaborate machinery that appeals to the rage-fear person. The sense of power felt when working on this perfection gives added prestige.

As the hand is the extension of the brain, so is the drive of rage an extension of the inner drive of love. Rage is just one stage in the passage of love from the state

of purpose in the mind to expression in the act of manifestation.

Martin Luther was of this type. The great truth that
electrified him and forced him to post his theses on the
door of the church at Wittenberg was the idea of justifica-
tion by faith. From this the Protestant Reformation
stemmed. Faith alone even without the works was enough
for salvation.

But in his own life Luther did not live as he professed,
for his whole life was one of action or works. His faith
led him to good act after courageous act. He was a prodigious doer, a worker of great capacity. His life was one
of good works. He was of the stuff of which martyrs are
made.

One of the greatest geniuses of all time was of this
type, Michelangelo. Admitted by all as beyond compare
as an artist, he worked with the utmost vigor all his ninety
years and died in harness. He is the man who, of all men,
most nearly approached the inner sense of perfection
he felt within him. This is what kept him at his great work
for so many years. Maybe perfection itself, or the absolute
was not for him, but he would make a tremendous try
for it.

The frescoes of the "Last Judgment," on the ceiling
of the Sistine Chapel, are the greatest in the world, a
concept of vast proportions, done with a technique that
had no flaws. It is a stark and terrible picture he gives of
the hopelessness of man and human destiny in the face
of fate. But for pure power in the painting there is nothing
like it.

It took him four years to complete the work. And all
this time he lay on his back clad in a loincloth. For some

time after he had finished he walked around with his head stretched backward.

He, too, was of the stuff of which martyrs are made. His vision of perfection never let him alone. He was a giant who would give all he had for the unveiling of that perfection. And from the finite standpoint he accomplished it.

In this day and age we can say that we have witnessed the life and deeds of one of the greatest rage-fear types in all history. That is the life and death of Mahatma Gandhi. In him this profound desire for perfection found a fervent acolyte.

In the early part of his life he was a very successful lawyer, making big money. There was no question of the practical capacity of his mind. But his inner drive was to help his fellow Indians whom he saw persecuted in Africa. So the great man was forced to give up the life of the law and devote himself to the service of suffering mankind.

Here was another martyr, and he did die a martyr's death. But I am sure Gandhi never considered himself one. He was always ready to forgive the violent people who ignorantly opposed him. He certainly in later life approached as near to spiritual perfection as finite man can. There was no limit to the love he felt for the poor and unfortunate of the world.

Gandhi represents what method and procedure can do to bring to earth and manifestation a great spiritual idea. He not only conceived the idea of freedom for the Indian people, but he evolved the way by which it could come about. His policy of passive resistance, of spiritual non-violence, brought about India's freedom. This was accomplished in such a way that there was relatively little animosity aroused among the British. They were sporting enough to recognize fair play in another. Surely the relations between India and England are infinitely more friendly than they would have been had force been used. Gandhi gave us a picture of the God within man as few individuals have in such perfection.

We call the rage-fear type the engineer. But we mean the engineer of the spirit as well as of matter. It all depends upon the plane of life of the individual. For there is spiritual efficiency as well as physical. And the application of spiritual methods can change history.

Gladstone, Oliver Cromwell and Anthony Comstock are in the rage-fear classification.

THE RAGE DRIVE
SUMMARY

ENERGY, MECHANICAL SENSE, CONSTRUCTIVE
URGE—NOT ANGER

ACCENT ON METHOD AND PROCEDURE—OBJECTIVE
CREATIVITY

THE ENGINEER IN ALL FIELDS

WANTS TO CHANGE PHYSICAL ENVIRONMENT

AGGRESSIVE—POSITIVE QUALITY WHEN USED AGAINST
NATURE OR FOR OTHER MEN

DOERS RATHER THAN THINKERS—"LET'S GET GOING!"

JOINERS—LIKE PEOPLE IN GROUPS—OFTEN POPULAR

CYCLOID INTROVERTS

EMOTIONAL REACTIONS DELAYED

LOGICAL REASON

CONTROLLED ASSOCIATION

LIKE ROUTINE

PREFER TO WORK WITH OTHERS

RAGE-SEX

The Financier—*I have Common Sense* the watchword

Deliberative—slow decisions

Wants to change physical environment to make more efficient, but resists change in social and economic life

Likes bigness—earth movers, bankers, executives

Never gives up

Handles people well

Humor ingenuous, childlike

Dependable and solid

RAGE-WONDER

The Mechanic—*I analyze*

Adaptive—makes up mind quickly but doesn't speak until he knows what others want

Work, Work, Work keynote

Likes machinery, especially in motion

Analyzes and classifies, gathers statistics

Interested in detail

Orderly and thorough; exact

Completely trustworthy; handle estates, etc.

Shrewd; often dry and brittle

Faithful friend; steadfast

RAGE-FEAR

The Engineer—*I maneuver*

Imperative will; quick decisions

Self-controlled, logical, sensible, accurate

Capable of great heights and depths of feeling. Can become martyr.

Inner drive for perfection makes him seem competitive

Ambitious; inner drive for success, power

Mountain-climber—gets to top

Likes intricate machinery—watch-making, electronics, etc.

Trouble-shooter

Devises selling schemes

Makes good lawyer, civil servant, politician

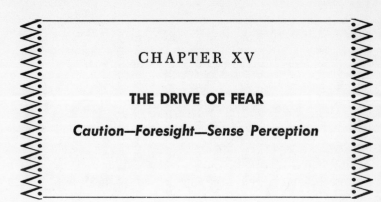

CHAPTER XV

THE DRIVE OF FEAR

Caution—Foresight—Sense Perception

When an animal is faced with a situation dangerous to its survival, it takes one of two courses. It fights in anger or it retreats in fear. The two drives of *rage* and *fear* are therefore the two ways that man reacts to physical danger. He becomes aggressive and fights to change the situation, as in rage, or he thinks about the danger and decides to retreat from it. *Anger* is his first reaction and is entirely without thought. *Fear* is the second reaction and is arrived at after the process of thought.

In neurosis also the same principle holds. The disturbing experience in childhood is either fought against aggressively, or run away from in *fear*.

Fear is the drive of caution, foresight, looking ahead into the future and taking the steps necessary to counteract the problems in the way of a course of action. It is strong in sense perception. And the people of this type always betray the fact that they have one of the five senses especially well-developed.

Fear is positive in that it helps to protect the body. It

is part of the objective means by which we save ourselves from danger. It was undoubtedly the emotion of fear that caused men to gather together in groups. These later became towns and cities which were used as a means of protection from animals and dangerous enemies. Therefore we can say that *fear* was the instrumental cause of the beginnings of all civilizations.

Your sense of fear has saved your life many times. For instance, it has caused you to run from an oncoming automobile often. It has saved you from falling on the ice by making you extra cautious when the sidewalks were slippery. Over and over again it has protected your life. So we can say that the drive is one of safeguarding, taking care of, protecting things.

In everyone's life the drive of fear is of the utmost importance. Caution is always thinking about the best and safest way of doing things. It is pointing out to the more impulsive creative drive, for instance, that the wise way to do a thing is this way, not that. It directs and guides and tries always to find the way of safety.

Apparently the only fears the baby has are those produced by a loud noise or by the feeling of falling. All his later fears are those produced by his experience in life. As he listens to the fears and prohibitions of his parents he learns the many fears he exhibits in his later life.

Beyond the safety of the individual, the drive of fear provides for the safety of the herd, for man is a herd animal and his safety depends on the safety of the herd. Every man has the emotion of fear but in the fear type its qualities are specially accented.

There are countless ways in which this great drive of foresight, looking ahead, caution, is necessary in life.

How could a man construct a complicated machine without the quality of foresight? He has to be able to visualize the fact that if he does this, then that effect will eventuate. If he does something else it will cause another effect.

Once a creative idea is thought of it is necessary to think about how it can be put into practical form. And here the rage and the fear drives are of the utmost necessity. For they are the drives that produce actual manifestation. They take the blueprint of the idea and put it into exact physical form. Without the sense of caution all sorts of foolish, impractical ideas might get into form.

No instinct that God puts into us is without use. Rage and fear together are the drives to protect physical life. Rage does it by fighting, fear by caution or retreat. When they are sublimated as they are in the emotional drives, they still have as basic urge the protection of the physical life forces.

The fear drive, like the rage drive, is basically interested in method and procedure, the processes of doing things. And so with its drive of sense perception it is always interested in how to get the blueprint into actual form.

We take the businessman as the great example of the drive of fear. This man likes to trade, and knows the value of what he trades in. He is the banker or the insurance man, both of whom take care of your money or your possessions. He is likely to be the man who writes down the history of the town in which he lives. He is the one who makes collections of objects—glass, china, silver, old furniture. He loves these objects so much that he desires to own them and protect them.

Our libraries and our museums are the products of this drive to protect the great works of civilization. Today we can enter the Metropolitan Museum in New York and see all the finest aspirations of Greece, Egypt and Rome spread out before our eyes. And we owe this to the drive of fear.

In the Museum of Natural History we see the protection of all the knowledge the race has acquired of animal and early human life on the globe. It is of the utmost importance for us to have museums like these. They give us an invaluable picture of past life, or they show us aspects of our world we do not know.

Wall Street used to be called the street of fear. Every time a rumor hit it the stocks would go up or down. This is the bankers' street where all the industry of America is traded in. And its principle characteristic is caution, foresight, looking ahead, and trading in futures. It protects physical America.

Fear is the nurture instinct in higher form. It trades so that food may be given to all, so that goods may flow to all who need them. Trade now is no longer barter, but it is a complicated form of exchange of goods for labor, nevertheless. It is the trading desire highly developed today.

The family was the first herd or horde. Families stayed together for protection. Out of this developed the village, the town, the state, and the nation as the need for protection grew. Today it is the council of fear that is urging us to see to it that we have a world government. For we realize now that in no other way can the safety of the world be assured.

Another caution idea is the idea of law and the police system. It is designed for the protection of the great body of citizens from the attacks of the irrational few who practice violence. And now today we are beginning to see the absolute necessity for a world police force to keep order among nations.

For our fear tells us that some irrational dictator may arise suddenly, in violent mood, plunge the world into atomic war. Without this quality of caution or foresight we would not bother to prepare for the dangers which can arise.

The fear drive is responsible for our hospitals. For they are manifestly a caretaking endeavor. They help to protect life, fight disease, try to find new methods of combatting the problem of human sickness. All the drives, sex, wonder, rage, and fear are enlisted in the battle to control disease. Each drive furnishes its particular ability. But it is fear that starts the whole process in motion.

What is the idea of government but a fear idea? The whole reason for government is to take care of people, to pass laws for their safety and welfare. The President of the United States is the servant of the people. He is dedicated to keeping them safe and in peace. Keeping order in town, country and world is the high duty of the drive of fear.

The Secretary of the Treasury is sometimes called its watchdog. His main job is the regulation of all fiscal policies. His aim is to keep business in operation, avoiding panics, keeping the business cycle on an even keel. He guards the financial structure of the country. He protects the American standard of living.

The Constitution of the United States was first of all a creation of love and creativity, a new concept of government. But its basic reason for being was the maintenance of order in the United States.

So perhaps you begin to see the importance of this great human drive of fear. You might say that it is the final step in the progress of a creative idea after it is first taken from the blue. The second step is the interpretive drive of wonder when the actual blueprint is made. Rage then takes over and puts the blueprint into form. Then fear finances, guards, and sells the product.

The average fear types are everywhere in life. They are lawyers, bankers, insurance men, traders, big and small. Because their sense perceptions are so strong, they handle objective things better than others. If it is ideas they are handling, these ideas are on the factual side. They know value and are not likely to be fooled in a trade.

They like routine work and can both give and take orders. They enjoy work in large organizations. They feel a certain sense of prestige in working for United States Steel, or Macy's or the Metropolitan Life Insurance Company.

They are always looking ahead, discounting the future. They are in real estate, in manufacturing of all sorts, exporting and importing. They are the little people who work all day long in small stores. They are also the big operators. They have a good money sense and are fine at statistics etcetera.

They are more likely to print the newspapers than to gather the news. They are the salesmen who know the value of the product they sell and are able to convince others. They are experts in the food and drink trades. This type, together with the rage type, has had most to do with changing the face of this country.

The surgeon with his accurate sight, his accurate sense

of touch, his accurate sense perception, on which may hang the life of his patient, is often of this drive.

This is the realist of realists. He is generally a hard-headed practical man, a solid member of the community. The type reasons logically, his mind working by controlled association. That is, he knows step by step how he arrives at his conclusion. He sees everything as it is on the surface, and this means people as well as things. He is not so apt to look for meaning in what he sees. He accepts people at their face value without too much questioning.

When he is highly endowed subjectively he is still the realist at work. He sees every detail, and employs sense imagery that is aware of every part of the scene. Walt Whitman is a good example of the type on a subjective plane.

The love or creative drive is not able to protect itself. This drive does so ably. Together with rage it goes to work to make the external situation possible for the unfolding of the love drive.

CHAPTER XVI

THE FEAR-SEX TYPE

Cautious—Creative

When we say that the *fear* types are the realists of realists, we mean that their accent is based on the keenest possible uses of the physical senses. These senses of sight, hearing, touch, taste, and smell introduce us to the mysteries of our three dimensional existence here on earth. Through them we touch the world in which we live and the phenomena of the world touch us.

Every sense is in reality a sense of touch. Quite evidently your hand touches all it meets. But so do little invisible particles of matter touch the lining of your nose, causing you the experience of smell. These particles are floating in the air.

The taste buds in your mouth are touched by particles of matter in the saliva. The ear is touched by waves of sound coming through the atmosphere. And your eye, the most important sense organ of all, is touched by waves of light coming through the air.

The sense part of the mind is the mind of the body. It is the most exterior part of the mind but it is of great importance. The more accurately and keenly our senses are developed, the more accurate is our view of the reality of our world. All later inner sense perception and ability to see meaning are based on this first view of the world we get through our sense mind.

The *fear-sex* type therefore is a combination of caution, foresight, and sense perception, modified by creativity or nurture. It is a *caution-love* union. While the love gives it its manner of action, the caution is its center of being.

So this is a very loving type, with its love centering on the home. It is a gentle, quiet, tender, sympathetic, protective type. In a nutshell, the *caution* holds the *love* to the region of the home. The type will do almost anything to keep the home together.

A woman of this type was married to a man who became violent in the course of his psychosis. Almost any other type would have been glad to be free of this constant menace of physical danger. But this woman did not want to be free. She underwent a great deal of agony to keep the home together. Happy or not, she wanted her home.

Seabury says that domesticity is the product of fear and sex. And this type is an example of his statement. The type works for the home, saves for the home. Nothing fills them with such joy as the family spirit they are able to engender. Family parties, children coming to dinner on Sundays, mean more to this type than any other entertainment.

' So it is not surprising that people of this type, when they go into business, find their greatest interest to be in manufacturing or dealing in something that has to do with the home. There they are in the furniture business, in the kitchen equipment field. They will be found manufacturing all the million gadgets which are apparently necessary for modern living. They are in television, radio, wallpaper, paints, fabrics for the home. You will find them in the clothing business, making beautiful gowns for the home. Their fine sense perception is most important in the styling of all these things.

Christian Dior was a man of this type. He was very decided and imperative. His mind was quick. He always knew instinctively what was correct for any lady. Here's what he had to say at the opening of one of his style shows in New York. "I listen for a certain quality in the silence." This is the realist at work sensing approval of disapproval. Then he emitted this gem of realistic thinking. "The women who are the loudest for the short skirt will soon be wearing the longest dresses."

Since the home must have food and drink, this type goes into such work. They are the butchers and grocers, the tea and coffee importers. They become the great cooks, whose sense of taste and smell are so well-developed. They enjoy nuances of flavor and aroma and often become gourmets.

Environment makes a strong impression on these people. They are responsive to it. And so because they like the familiar, they do not move around much. Once they are happily situated they are more likely to travel by subscribing to the *National Geographic*.

The great department stores are examples of how this type is interested in merchandising for the home. It was no accident that John Wanamaker was the proprietor of the first department store, for he was of this type.

The minds of the drive are quick and imperative. They are able, however, to keep this pretty well under control usually. Their love helps them here. But in questions of the home and family they can become a little arbitrary.

I think the term trader is a very good one for them. They know the quality of the goods they deal in extremely well. They have foresight and caution and a fine sense of money values. They enjoy the give and take of the usual trade.

The backbone of many a farm family will be found to be of this type. They are extremely tenacious in holding on to anything they want. And they can be tenacious in keeping on with a long, laborious job until it is finished. It is almost impossible to stop them from doing what they set out to do. Long after others have given up a job as hopeless, this type will still be holding on with grim tenacity.

Kipling was of this type. In his early work you can see the man of sense perception. In the *Jungle Books* he shows great sensitivity to the ways of animals in nature. Keen observation is here, an exquisite awareness of the habits of wild life.

Then later in life he had great success. And in conformity with what often happens with the type, he became conservative and an imperialist. And no one will say that his remarks on America betrayed the fact that he possessed sensitivity.

There are those of high and low planes of feeling and thought in all types. But since this is psycho-synthesis we are explaining, we spend our time with those on the higher planes. And this is because the higher planes gives us a better picture of the possibilities of the type.

Walt Whitman had this drive. He was a realist living always in the phenomenal world. He was in the world and of the world. And yet his nature was on such a scale of genius that he transcended the type.

Yet always he used sense imagery with great effect.
The lilacs bloom by the dooryard, the juicy autumnal fruit
is ripe and red from the orchard. The pioneers are from
the peaks gigantic, from the great sierras and the high
plateaus. He sees everything, he feels everything, he is
continually sensing the life and the objects around him.

But how deeply subjective the man can become. By
constant reiteration of his sense imagery we feel below the
words the deep subjective emotion. Here is a piece from
A Song of Joys.

O to make the most jubilant song
Full of music—full of manhood, womanhood, infancy,
Full of common employments—full of grain and trees.

O for the voice of animals—O for the swiftness and
*   balance of fishes,*
O for the dropping of raindrops in a song
O for the sunshine and motion of waves in a song.

What a subjective picture of joy and power and life
and song he is able to evoke in these few lines of wonderful
sense imagery!

You do not get from Whitman the self-analysis of the
more introspective types. He does not give you, nor can
he, the subtle distinctions that a man like William Blake
makes. But he does give you the robust feeling of a man of
the earth, seeing, feeling, sensing the joys and beauties
of his environment. And he can express spiritual ideas too,
as when he says that there is more to a man than can be
seen between his hat and his boots.

Whitman was a great man. He was comprehensive.

There is much more in his poetry than appears in the literal reading. He celebrated his home, America, in words that will be heard down the corridors of time.

With the love encouraging the fear to be true to itself in so many ways, it is no wonder that this type does not progress very far from the home. Fear naturally does not want to leave home, and the love provides the excitement necessary in the family group. And also the tenacious quality comes in to buttress up the fortress of the home. Once a fear type has been moved to love a mate, that mate has only a Chinaman's chance of ever getting away. These are the stable people. They are the certain members of the community. They are always there, they can always be counted upon. They will never let down the town or the group in any way.

I protect is a fitting phrase to describe these people.

The *fear-sex* classification also includes Anatole France and Thomas Carlyle.

CHAPTER XVII

THE FEAR-WONDER TYPE

Cautious—Interpretive

We have here the drive of *caution, foresight, sense perception* modified by *wonder,* the drive of interpretation, the drive for meaning. In certain combinations this causes the caution to go deep, but in other natures it drives them horizontally and not so deep. These latter seek ever new outlets for the protective drive of *fear.*

The type is therefore able to develop a chameleon-like quality of being all things to all men. They take on the coloring of their surroundings, as does the chameleon, for protection. With gay people they can be gay, with the grave they can be grave. They are so sympathetic, particularly when the wonder drives the attention deep, that they are able to feel sympathy as few people can. This is a wonderful quality in human relations. And so, as you would expect, these people are very successful in their contacts with others. They exude a sympathy which everyone feels. They make you certain that they like you. This quality adds greatly to the felicity of life.

The result of these qualities is that they often become

fine actors. They can take on the feeling of a part with utmost ease. They can be slapstick like Ed Wynn, losing themselves in the humor of the situation they are evoking. They are gentle, never biting, as a comic such as Groucho Marx can be. Marx is a sex-fear type, with great wit and a rapier-like mind. The *fear-wonder* types, as comics, never go very deep. They are not interested in ideas. They are interested in the people and things around them.

The activity pattern of wonder, when it is combined with fear, and dominated by fear, means that the fear forbids the wonder to be free. It keeps attention close to the surface. In rare cases, it can become fixated on an idea. But usually the focus of attention turns back to the objective reality around it.

In almost all cases the mind concerns itself with things. Seldom does it indulge itself in phantasy, except in relation to human situations. And there it can well carry a phantasy image of unconsummated love for years. But it is not likely to carry the torch for an *idea* for very long.

The great English poet Keats was this type. He was, of course, on a pretty high plane, but his approach to his art was typical of the type's reaction. Listen to this music, gentle, fragile, delicate. It is the music of a mind that sees and feels with great sense perception. There are no ideas but beauty. He is in the scene, sensing it with utmost perception.

I stood tiptoe upon a little hill,
The air was cooling, and so very still,
That the sweet buds which with a modest pride
Pull droopingly, in slanting curve aside,
Their scantly leaved, and finely tapering stems,

Had not yet lost those starry diadems
Caught from the early sobbing of the morn.
The clouds were pure and white as flocks new shorn,
And fresh from the clear brook; sweetly they slept
On the blue fields of heaven, and then there crept
A little noiseless noise among the leaves,
Born of the sigh that silence heaves.

Surely this is a gem of sense imagery. And it goes deep into the scene. It tells you how the poet feels as he paints it for you from his palette of sound.

Naturally in a description of the types we strive to give most attention to the average. But it must never be forgotten that there are men and women on all planes of objectivity and subjectivity in each drive. This is why I have mentioned the artist in the fear type classifications. I don't want the reader to get the idea that artists only belong to a certain type. They simply take on, in their art, the particular bent of the special drive.

I serve is the phrase that best describes the type. While they do serve in many of the smaller jobs of life, that is not the whole of it. The ideal of being of service to mankind is the highest purpose man has. When one man turns to his brother with the attitude of trying to help and cooperate with him, that is a high spiritual position to take. It follows the second commandment of Jesus, to love the neighbor as the self. And the great Teacher said on another occasion that he who would be first in the kingdom is the man who ministers to his fellow men.

While seldom reaching this ideal, the fear-wonder type has the possibility of human service within its scope. It is quite possible that society is still so primitive that the kindliness and desire of the type to serve has been taken advantage of.

On the plane of modern business, for instance, service plays a most important role. The salesman knows today that he is, to a great extent, selling service when he sells a product. His product must do what he says it will. His company stands behind its product with service.

Also the salesman knows today that he does not have to enter a prospect's office in fear and trembling as was so often the case in the past. He knows that he has service to offer his client. So he feels that he will be welcome. A good sale is of benefit to both parties and this is the life of trade.

It can be said that the fear-wonder type is the salesman par excellence. He knows instinctively how others feel. He also knows that it is the feeling of the other man that must be appealed to when making the sale. The intellect is subsidiary to the feeling. Find out the love of the prospect—that is the way to sell him. And here the type is most successful. It can sense the feeling of the other. Being able to fall into the mood of the prospect is a very valuable asset in selling.

The type is adaptive. That means that it is always thinking of the other man. When the fear-wonder type presents an idea, he always thinks of the manner which will most please the other man.

Like the other fear types, the fear-wonder person likes to be associated with a large organization. He senses the power of the corporation, and basks in it.

The type will be found in welfare work and social work. They make wonderful nurses and doctors. Since they are so good in human relations, you will find them in many positions demanding this quality. They are successful in the hotel business, in public relations, as secretaries, receptionists, expediters, photographers, and so forth.

The minister who will never set the world afire as a preacher often finds himself acting as assistant to a man who *is* a great preacher, and only that. The fear-wonder person, with his special ability in human relations, takes on the pastoral work of the parish.

He is very much the realist, as the other fear types are. He is practical and logical. He is very much aware of his environment, and is greatly affected by those with whom he comes in contact.

But also, in some of the more evolved members of the type there is a dreamy quality. Their desire for mystic experience seems to contradict their practicality. Many Catholic women of the type become nuns, while men seek the priesthood. They do not reason out their bent in this direction. They simply love the occult and mysterious. The fact of the size and authority of the organized church also appeals to them.

Washington Irving was of this type. He was a realist, but he was also interested in all the strange and mysterious objects, scenes and events of the world. He lays bare his mind under the title, *The Author's Account of Himself*. He says, "I was always fond of visiting new scenes, and observing strange characters and manners. . . . My holiday afternoons were spent in rambles around the surrounding country. I made myself familiar with all its places famous in history or fable. I knew every spot where murder or robbery had been committed, or a ghost seen. . . . This rambling propensity strengthened with my years."

His wonder drove Irving to see all the famous places

of the world. His fear made him describe what he did and what he saw in an impersonal, unfeeling sort of way. You read his story and find the facts interesting, but you never feel the inside of his characters.

"Rip Van Winkle" is perhaps his most famous story. He has used an old Catskill tale as a base. But he tells the story without much feeling. His anecdote is interesting and that is all. He cannot communicate feeling, or he does not feel. In this he differs from Keats who feels deeply.

In Keats the wonder drives the fear deep into the subject. In Irving the wonder drives the fear to a search for excitement all over the world. One is horizontal, the other vertical, yet both are the same type.

The fear-wonder type is therefore the type of all others that can lose himself in service to others. Its descriptive phrase is, naturally, *I serve*. And this is why he has not produced so many famous individuals as yet. It is perhaps the least egocentric.

P. T. Barnum and Hamlet are included in this group.

CHAPTER XVIII

THE FEAR-RAGE TYPE

Cautious—Constructive

I determine is the phrase that best applies to this type. For its determination is very great. While there are more famous men and women in the *rage* group as a whole, I believe *fear-rage* has produced more than any other individual drive. There is great power in the type, which is proved by the number of people who have succeeded in all areas of life.

In this case *fear*, or the drive of caution, foresight, sense perception is modified by *rage*, or the drive of construction, mechanical sense, energy, the urge to build. The caution is driven on by a tremendous energy, while the energy is kept in bounds by the caution. So this type can be said to be the realist of realists, having the best and most accurate picture of the external world of any type.

It is a caution-courage combination. It was Napoleon, who was of this type, who said that the bravest men were those who were naturally the most fearful. And this type can determine to go through with a dangerous operation, doing it with cool courage, which is doubly dangerous because of the innate caution within.

There is, however, the same schism between the energy and the caution that appears in the rage-fear type, but this time reversed. When the caution is top-heavy it can keep the type from all action. Both fear and rage are outward tendencies. That is why the type is so much at home in its environment. It is not usually troubled with too many subjective ideas, and very much at ease with objects and facts.

Seabury says that the type is made searchingly alert by the activity of their fear and aggressively energetic by the initiative of their rage. They are singularly empowered to put through their purposes and often can display great concentration.

Since the caution is continually pushed on by the rage, you can see that the type is going to be very efficient. It is guided straight to its object, and it always knows what it is doing. We call this type the analyst because accuracy is one of its salient characteristics. But it is so broad in its interests that it is all over the map, doing every kind of work.

Napoleon showed the great genius of the type in warfare. Goethe displayed it in literature and science. Sir Isaac Newton was an example of the scientific accuracy of the mind.

Napoleon is the epitome of the type. He had great personal power, iron will and determination. His fear or caution gave him much exterior wisdom. He had a slow mind, as is characteristic of the type. He waited until all the evidence was in before coming to a decision. This made him the great strategist. Before he went into action he had a most realistic picture of the terrain, of the disposition of his troops and those of the enemy. His analysis of each situation was accurate and wise. His determination made him the conqueror.

Goethe was another towering world genius of this type. Like all genius he transcended the type. For usually the drive is most realistic and not very subjective. Goethe had both sides of his mind developed, the inner and the outer. He was both objective and subjective. He had a scientific bent and studied alchemy, physiognomy, the natural sciences, which were then in a state of great activity. He published two volumes on light and color. Also, at one time, he was a member of the Privy Council at Weimar, and served the state for a number of years.

But his main claim to fame is on the literary side. In poetry and drama he became a world figure. In his greatest work, *Faust*, he gave a living picture of the failure of man to live up to the possibilities of his spirit, the God within.

Physically we know that in the creation of the child, the man plants the seed in the woman. But in the creation of the psychic child of man, the work of art, it is the woman who impregnates the mind of the man with love for her. She stimulates him to his creation. This was especially true in the case of Goethe. He always needed the stimulation of a woman to get him going creatively, and so he was in a continual state of falling in love.

The type has great executive and political powers. They like people and get along well with others. They can do routine work, can give and receive orders. Their eyes are so keen that they see like eagles, and they love to perceive the secrets of others. Sometimes their eyes and ears are so penetrating they make others a little nervous. Even when they say nothing others feel their unspoken criticism.

They are in business everywhere, analyzing, classifying and criticizing. They think by controlled association. This method of knowing the steps by which they reached their conclusion makes them good in argument and able lawyers.

There are many engineers and scientific men in this grouping. They also become bankers and insurance men where their statistical bent serves them well. Some of the best surgeons are of this type. This is on account of their sense perception which enables them to see, touch, and hear with the greatest subtlety.

This type is better in dealing with objects and facts and procedures and processes than with people. While they can report accurately on the external actions of people, they do not understand so well what is going on in the people's minds. It takes a less realistic type for this. In the same way, the artist of the type tends to emphasize physical beauty and perfection. He cannot express so well the beauty that lies under the surface.

This is the sound, common-sense individual. He is not likely to be swayed by a fallacious idea. He will not be influenced much by the phoney enthusiasm of the crackpot.

Because they are so realistic, the mysterious side of life poses them a problem. They are drawn to it but are unable to use their reason on the subject. This makes them seek occult ideas and all kinds of so-called teachers of strange, hidden knowledge.

The type is interested in power and they are always

aware of position and competition in the world. They are willing to overcome great obstacles in their pursuit of power. They can discipline themselves, too. They greatly desire the concentration that leads to the high positions in the world.

This is a serious nature and usually does not exhibit much humor. They are too focussed on the facts and the objects of life, the truths of nature and science.

Thomas Edison was a nature of this type. He exemplifies it in the highest degree. He was the greatest inventor the world has ever seen. He was not so much the creator of the new, but the man of method and procedure, intent on the problem of making his idea work. So he never created a new idea, but he put into form any useful idea that came to his attention. The work of this one man has revolutionized the physical and economic life of this planet.

All he needed to set his love into action was to be posed a problem. Always before he started on a project, he would investigate whether there was a need for the product. He was not the one to embark on a project that nobody wanted. He was not *money* conscious so much as he was *use* conscious.

If others were failing with a project, or said that it could not be done, that was all Edison needed to set him off. He would show them. And he was the happiest of men because he was able to get his love into action all the time. His work was play to him, in the best sense of the term. He could never understand why other men felt the need of a vacation. All he asked was a knotty problem to get to work on.

His inventions, in whole or in part, have given the world

electric light and power, the phonograph, the storage battery, the radio, the dynamo, and literally hundreds of smaller inventions, down to waxed and gummed paper. His was an enormous practicality harnessed to great creative power. He never tackled anything unless he thought it had practical appeal. No pure science for him. Applied, useful science for him every time.

He said he investigated minutely the necessity for any particular invention before he started to spend time on it. He was the ingenious inventor who could, par excellence, apply a scientific truth to a practical end. He was true to his type, a man of method and procedure.

He had boundless energy and iron determination. And what a prodigious amount of work he accomplished! Once, during the years, he was experimenting on the storage battery. One of his assistants came to him and said, "Isn't it a shame, that with the tremendous amount of work you have done on the battery, you haven't been able to get any results?" "Results?," Edison smiled back at him, "Why, man, I've got a lot of results. I know several thousand things that won't work."

This was the man who never gave up. His work was play and he enjoyed every minute of it. He is a wonderful example of the type at its best.

The fear-rage type is one of enormous energy. Powerful, brilliant, it sees objects and events with great accuracy. It is closest to surface reality than any other type.

Among the many famous people who are included in it are Victor Hugo, Sir Isaac Newton, Rudolf Steiner, and Milton.

THE FEAR DRIVE
SUMMARY

ACCENT ON FORESIGHT, CAUTION, SENSE PERCEPTION

EXTERNAL WISDOM—ON OBJECTIVE SIDE OF LIFE

PROTECTIVE QUALITY—GUARDIANS

KNOW VALUES BETTER THAN ANY OTHER DRIVE

LIKE ROUTINE WORK

CAN BOTH GIVE AND TAKE ORDERS

REASONS LOGICALLY—CONTROLLED ASSOCIATION

LIKES TO WORK IN LARGE ORGANIZATIONS—NOT
LONE WOLF JOBS

REALIST OF REALISTS—HARD-HEADED, PRACTICAL

NOT PARTICULARLY INTERESTED IN MEANING—ACCEPTS
FACE VALUES

CYCLOID EXTRAVERT

EMOTIONAL REACTION DELAYED

FEAR-SEX

The Trader—*I protect*
Imperative will—quick decisions

Caution—love union
Love centers around home—domesticity
Gentle, quiet, tenderly sympathetic
Works for things related to home—farming, building, manufacturing, trading, etc.
More responsive to environment than average
Likes familiar things
Tenacious

FEAR-WONDER

The Salesman—*I serve*
Adaptive will—quick decision, slow action
Fear modified by curiosity.
Fear makes him want to know what other person thinks, to please him; wonder makes him "go with" other person. Chameleon-like quality.
Service watchword; when on high plane, the service of mankind
Most proficient in selling
Good mimic
Often exploited by powerful people because of his wish to serve

FEAR-RAGE

The Analyst—*I determine*
Deliberative will—slow reaction
Cautious—daring
Sense perception prominent characteristic
Doesn't seem fearful, but energy of rage drives him on
Very efficient—drives straight to goal
Statistical, analytical
Powerful, sometimes dominating
Keen foresight, ability to evaluate
Resists coercion.
Little humor, if any
Mystic, at heart—loves undercurrents
In business, science, inventions. Good surgeon.

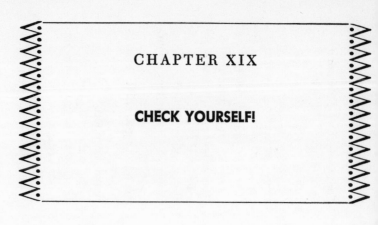

CHAPTER XIX

CHECK YOURSELF!

Well, now you have read descriptions of every man, woman and child in this old world! And among them you have found your own Self.

In order to check your findings, take the tests which follow. Remember, it is your first reaction to the question that is asked, your natural reaction, not the one your training-pattern has produced. What we are seeking is your true Self, the loves, abilities, capacities with which your Creator has endowed you. For only as you discover and develop your loves can you be truly happy and satisfied.

If the results of your tests do not entirely check with the type whose description you believe fits you, go over both description and tests again, with this point in mind: ask yourself, is this my *natural* reaction?

Some years ago Seabury had a client who seemed to be of a certain type. But she was never satisfied about it. Finally she came into contact with the nurse who had taken care of her when she was very small. From this woman she learned that her childhood reactions were completely different from those of her later years. It developed that she had had a very powerful mother, and had so taken on the mother's pattern that it seemed to be her own. The fact that she wasn't satisfied, however, with the type her mother's pattern had placed her in proved that it was not her own. Her new knowledge of herself changed her whole life as her true nature was liberated.

I was interested in reading lately of a man who held an important job in a big government agency. He resigned to give his whole time to painting. He has been fortunate enough to have found his love, and is following that star.

Now you, too, can reach for your particular star, and find it!

THE CYCLOID—SCHIZOID CLASSIFICATION
DOER OR THINKER?

	a	b

1. When you hear news that will make you sad or happy,
    a. does it take some time before it "gets" you—before you feel the emotion?
    or
    b. do you feel the emotion immediately?		

2. a. Would you rather go places and do things with people than sit home with a book?
    or
    b. Do you get restless if you have to be with people for a long time?		

3. a. Do you like to follow the same schedule every day—get up at the same time, have meals on the dot, et cetera?
    or
    b. Do you rebel at doing the same thing the same way over and over?		

4. a. Do you get restless if you have to stick at one thing very long?
    or
    b. If you're interested in a job, can you stick at it for a long time without feeling the need of a "break?"		

CHECK ONE
a   b

5. a. Can you give orders as well as take them?
      or
  b. Do you dislike to take orders from anyone, advice as to how you should do a job, et cetera?

6. a. Do you always know why you believe as you do, and are you always able to give your reasons?
      or
  b. Do you have strong convictions on many subjects, but in an argument are not always able to give your reasons?

7. a. Do you think a person isn't in his right mind if he turns down a job with a bigger salary than he's getting because he doesn't like the work involved?
      or
  b. Is it important to you to work at some thing you like, even though you might earn more at something else?

8. a. Does it irritate you to hear people talk a lot about theories—you wish they'd get down to facts?
      or
  b. Are ideas more important to you than facts and objects?

9. a. Is "common sense" the only thing that makes sense to you?
      or
  b. Is "common sense" more common than sense to you?

	a	b
10. a. Do you like to own things? *or* b. Does it seem unimportant to you to own things, except what you need, or what satisfies your love of beauty?		
11. a. Other things being equal, do you prefer business to a profession? *or* b. Do you prefer a professional career to business?		
12. a. Do you have a great many friends, and enjoying partying with them? *or* b. Do you tend to enjoy a few friends, rather than a host of acquaintances?		
13. a. Do you think experience is the best teacher? *or* b. Do you believe that you can't judge the future by the past?		
14. a. Do people, objects or circumstances stimulate your ideas? *or* b. Do your ideas seem to come to you out of the blue, without outside stimulation?		
15. a. Do you take pride in being practical, "hard-headed"? *or* b. Do so-called practical people sometimes seem to you to lack imagination?		

If you have a majority of checks in the (a) column, you are a cycloid.

If you have a majority of checks in the (b) column, you are a schizoid.

YOUR *WILL* TYPE

	CHECK ONE		
	a	b	c
1. When a problem is presented to you, do you			
a. know immediately what you think, and go into action at once?			
b. have to take time to consider what you think—weigh all the evidence before you speak?			
c. know immediately what you think, but wait to speak or act until you know how others react?			
2. When you have a piece of work to do, do you			
a. immediately have a plan and start to work on it? And sometimes find that you have to revise what you've done, or make some changes?			
b. take some time to think about possible plans, what you need in the way of materials, and finally start to work?			
c. begin promptly, feeling your way as the work develops, possibly improvising, but always being aware of everything around you?			

3. How do you react to other people?
    a. Do you often find that others are slow to grasp an explanation or a situation?
    b. Do you think many people go off half-cocked, make snap decisions, not taking time to really think anything out?
    c. Do you wish people would take the middle of the road—that some of them wouldn't speak and act so quickly, and that others wouldn't take so long to make up their minds?

4. How do others react to you?
    a. Do you have trouble in human relations, without having the slightest idea why? Are you considered "bossy"?
    b. Do people get impatient with you for taking so long to make up your mind? Are you sometimes thought stubborn?
    c. Are you considered easy to get along with, and generally successful in human relations? But in tending to agree, to say *yes* too easily, then wish you hadn't, do you sometimes upset other people's plans?

5. If you have a strong feeling that something is right, do you
    a. find it hard to believe that everyone else doesn't see immediately how right it is?
    b. resist changing your opinion, having come to your decision through weighing all the evidence?
    c. find at first that you are swayed by the

	CHECK ONE		
	a	b	c

opposite opinion, so that you don't put up a good argument, even though underneath you are still convinced that you are right?

6. If you feel that a certain course is just, and another person opposes you, what is your reaction?
   a. Do you rebut his argument immediately and passionately?
   b. Do you rebut his argument firmly but without so much feeling?
   c. Do you feel at first that there is something in what the other says, then make your rebuttal in as conciliatory a way as possible?

7. When you are involved in a project, do you
   a. see just one solution, concentrate on that, and see no alternative?
   b. see so many possible solutions that it takes you some time to make up your mind how to proceed?—But once your mind is made up, you are determined in pursuing your course?
   c. start out thinking one solution is right, but can be swayed by suggestion to another solution?

8. Suppose you were a commanding general in a campaign. Would you
   a. be able to adjust quickly to any change in conditions of battle, realign your forces to cope with new circumstances, as Patton and Montgomery could and did?

	CHECK ONE		
	a	b	c
b. be better at long-range strategy, but thrown off somewhat by a need to change your plan suddenly, as Jefferson said Washington was?			
c. feel that the essential of leadership was to have all the members of your staff working in complete harmony, believing that only so could the war be won, as Eisenhower did?			

INTERPRETATION

If you have a majority of checks in the (a) column, your will is *imperative*.

If you have a majority of checks in the (b) column, your will is *deliberative*.

If you have a majority of checks in the (c) column, your will is *adaptive*.

YOUR BASIC EMOTIONAL DRIVE

A

	YES	NO
1. Do you feel that you are a better judge of values than most people?		
2. Do you feel that you have a realistic view of life—that a fact is a fact, and it's a waste of time to talk about what something means, or what is behind the action of some person?		
3. Are you always looking ahead, trying to figure out how to proceed so that your plans will work out?		

	YES	NO

4. Do you tend to be apprehensive of possible danger in a situation or condition, and try to guard against it?

5. Are you especially aware of subtle differences in taste, odors, colors, textures, tones?

X. 6. Do you feel great sympathy for others?

7. Is your home the center of your life?

8. Would you rather work in some field related to the home than in anything else—food, furniture, farming, etcetera?

9. Do you hang on to what you have?

10. Have you an imperative will?

11. Does *I protect* describe the way you feel?

Y. 12. Do you always want to be of service in some way?

13. Would you make a good salesman?

14. Are you gay with gay people, sad with sad ones?—In other words, do you take on the color of your surroundings, like a chameleon?

15. Do others sometimes "use" you for their benefit, because of your desire to serve?

16. Is your will adaptive?

17. Does *I serve* describe you quite well?

Z. 18. If you start a project, do you drive straight ahead until you finish it?

19. Are you generally considered very efficient?

20. Do you rebel against being coerced into doing something you haven't chosen yourself?

21. Are you interested in the occult, the mysterious?

	YES	NO
22. Is your will deliberative?		
23. Does *I determine* describe your inner feeling?		

B

	YES	NO
1. Do you tend to get bored by the way things are arranged in your home or office, and feel the urge to change them?		
2. If you don't like a situation, do you feel impelled to do something about it—and generally act?		
3. Do you like to construct things—houses, furniture, dresses, soups?		
4. Have you a mechanical bent—interested in fixing things, or rearranging parts of a machine to make it more efficient?		
5. Do you tend to resist, if others try to make you change your mind?		

	YES	NO
X. 6. Do you resist change in your social and economic life?		
7. Do you prefer to work on large-scale projects rather than small ones—building roads, running a business, etc.?		
8. Do you like to handle money, as a banker, for instance?		
9. Would you say you handle people well?		
10. Is your will deliberative?		
11. Is *I have* a good description of the way you feel?		

	YES	NO
Y. 12. Do you find yourself always working at something?		
13. Do you like machinery in motion—planes, trains, cars?		

	YES	NO

14. Do you naturally analyze and classify facts that come to your attention?
15. Do you consider yourself a faithful friend?
16. Is your will adaptive?
17. Does *I analyze* describe you pretty well?

Z. 18. Do you experience great heights and depths of feeling?
19. Do you feel the urge to achieve perfection in all areas?
20. Do you like intricate machinery, such as watches, radios, etc?
21. Do you want to get to the top—climb mountains, and/or achieve business success, professional success?
22. Is your will imperative?
23. Does *I maneuver* describe you?

C

1. Are you always interested in knowing why and how events occur, how things are made, why people act as they do, etc.?
2. Do you always want to know the meaning behind events?
3. Are you interested in symbology—the meaning of symbols in myths, in dreams, in the Bible?
4. Do you feel a kinship with any kind of scientist —in natural science, atomic science, electronics, etcetera, or the scientist in human relations, as Woodrow Wilson was, or the scientist of the soul, like Emerson?
5. If you see some part of an object, all by itself, do you try to figure out what the original object was from which it came?

	YES	NO

X. 6. Do you find that you'd rather get to the bottom of one subject than know a little about a lot of things?

7. Do you feel you never know enough?

8. Are you interested in people, and anxious to help them with their social problems?

9. Do you feel that you know how to get people together who will be congenial?

10. Is your will deliberative?

11. Would you say that *I perceive* is a good description of you?

Y. 12. Do you feel you'd like to know more about practically everything?

13. Are you a good conversationalist?

14. Do you like to arouse people by giving them new ideas?

15. Do you yearn to explore the world?

16. Is your will adaptive?

17. Does *I investigate* describe you?

Z. 18. Is harmony a prime requisite for your happiness? Both in your physical surroundings and in human relations?

19. Is beauty essential to you?

20. Have you a strong sense of justice?

21. Are you able to adjust to new situations easily?

22. Is your will imperative?

23. Does *I balance* describe you?

D

1. Do you resist doing anything in the prescribed way? Do you react against old ideas?

	YES	NO
2. In analyzing your reaction to an idea, would you say that, more than most people, you pay attention to the emotional stimulus?		
3. Are you always trying to find some completely new idea or form of expression?		
4. Would you rather evolve new ideas than carry them out?		
5. Have you ever painted a picture, written a story or poem, composed music, or produced any other form of art? If not, do you feel a strong wish that you could?		

		YES	NO
X.	6. Do you love to teach, to explain?		
	7. Do you have a strong urge to find the meaning of life?		
	8. Do you generally want to do what others want?		
	9. Does physical order mean little or nothing to you, but spiritual order mean a great deal?		
	10. Is your will adaptive?		
	11. Does *I understand* describe your attitude toward life?		

		YES	NO
Y.	12. Do people choose you as a leader—president, chairman, etcetera?		
	13. Do you like to be in familiar surroundings —as a cat usually returns to the house he has known?		
	14. Do you like to work on large projects rather than detailed ones?		
	15. Do you have a strong sense of the dramatic?		
	16. Is your will deliberative?		
	17. Does *I command* describe your inner feeling?		

	YES	NO
Z. 18. Do you have very strong convictions?		
19. Do you carry the torch for your ideas—have a strong urge to convince others of them?		
20. Do you find that you stimulate others—excite them either for or against you?		
21. Do you have a sharp wit, that can sometimes be devastating to others?		
22. Is your will imperative?		
23. Does *I am* seem a fair description of your inner attitude?		

BASIC EMOTIONAL DRIVE

INTERPRETATION

Count the number of YES answers in each group, A, B, C, D.
In which group do you have the majority of "YES Answers"
If in A, your primary drive is FEAR OR SENSE PERCEPTION
If in B, your primary drive is RAGE OR THE CONSTRUCTIVE URGE
If in C, your primary drive is WONDER OR THE INTERPRETIVE SENSE
If in D, your primary drive is SEX OR CREATIVITY.

Now go back to the test in which you had the majority of
YES answers. Check the number of YES answers in each group,
X, Y, and Z. This will give you your specific emotional type.

AX—FEAR-SEX: SENSE PERCEPTION—CREATIVITY
AY—FEAR-WONDER: SENSE PERCEPTION—INTERPRETIVE SENSE
AZ—FEAR-RAGE: SENSE PERCEPTION—CONSTRUCTIVE URGE

BX—RAGE-SEX: CONSTRUCTIVE—CREATIVE
BY—RAGE-WONDER: CONSTRUCTIVE—INTERPRETIVE
BZ—RAGE-FEAR: CONSTRUCTIVE—SENSE PERCEPTION

CX—WONDER-FEAR: INTERPRETIVE—SENSE PERCEPTION
CY—WONDER-RAGE: INTERPRETIVE—CONSTRUCTIVE
CZ—WONDER-SEX: INTERPRETIVE—CREATIVE

DX—SEX-WONDER: CREATIVE—INTERPRETIVE
DY—SEX-RAGE: CREATIVE—CONSTRUCTIVE
DZ—SEX-FEAR: CREATIVE—SENSE PERCEPTION

Now go back over your findings and check them against the table on the next page. If you find a discrepancy, check your answers to be sure that they apply to what you do *naturally*, not what your experience has produced. For example, many imperative people have learned to hesitate before going into action. But *naturally*, they react imperatively.

CYCLOID-SCHIZOID	WILL	BASIC DRIVE	SPECIFIC TYPE	
SCHIZOID INTROVERT	IMPERATIVE	SEX	SEX-FEAR	CREATIVE-SENSE PERCEPTION
	DELIBERATIVE	,,	SEX-RAGE	CREATIVE-CONSTRUCTIVE
	ADAPTIVE	,,	SEX-WONDER	CREATIVE-INTERPRETIVE
SCHIZOID EXTRAVERT	IMPERATIVE	WONDER	WONDER-SEX	INTERPRETIVE-CREATIVE
	DELIBERATIVE	,,	WONDER-FEAR	INTERPRETIVE-SENSE PERCEPTION
	ADAPTIVE	,,	WONDER-RAGE	INTERPRETIVE-CONSTRUCTIVE
CYCLOID INTROVERT	IMPERATIVE	RAGE	RAGE-FEAR	CONSTRUCTIVE-SENSE PERCEPTION
	DELIBERATIVE	,,	RAGE-SEX	CONSTRUCTIVE-CREATIVE
	ADAPTIVE	,,	RAGE-WONDER	CONSTRUCTIVE-INTERPRETIVE
CYCLOID EXTRAVERT	IMPERATIVE	FEAR	FEAR-SEX	SENSE PERCEPTION-CREATIVE
	DELIBERATIVE	,,	FEAR-RAGE	SENSE PERCEPTION-CONSTRUCTIVE
	ADAPTIVE	,,	FEAR-WONDER	SENSE PERCEPTION-INTERPRETIVE